THE LIBRARIAN'S
GUIDE TO
LEARNING
THEORY

THE LIBRARIAN'S GUIDE TO **LEARNING THEORY**

PRACTICAL APPLICATIONS IN LIBRARY SETTINGS

ANN MEDAILLE

CHICAGO | 2024

ANN MEDAILLE is the director of research and instructional services at the University of Nevada, Reno Libraries, and serves as editor-in-chief of the journal *Evidence Based Library and Information Practice.* She has published several journal articles on topics related to educational theories and pedagogies. She also coauthored the book *Visual Literacy for Libraries: A Practical, Standards-Based Guide.*

Extensive effort has gone into ensuring the reliability of the information in this book; however, the publisher makes no warranty, express or implied, with respect to the material contained herein.

ISBN: 978-0-8389-3958-1 (paper)

Library of Congress Cataloging-in-Publication Data

Names: Medaille, Ann, author.
Title: The librarian's guide to learning theory : practical applications in library settings / Ann Medaille.
Description: Chicago : ALA Editions, 2024. | Includes bibliographical references and index. | Summary: "This book is intended to help librarians better understand how people learn and it reviews theories related to learning so that librarians can better support learning. The practical guidance offered in this book shows how librarians can apply these theories to library instruction, spaces, services, resources, and technologies"—Provided by publisher.
Identifiers: LCCN 2023021884 | ISBN 9780838939581 (paperback)
Subjects: LCSH: Libraries and education. | Learning—Philosophy. | Learning, Psychology of. | Library orientation. | Public services (Libraries) | Libraries and students.
Classification: LCC Z718 .M38 2023 | DDC 025.5—dc23/eng/20230710
LC record available at https://lccn.loc.gov/2023021884

Book design by Kim Hudgins in the Chaparral, Tisa Pro, and Proxima Nova typefaces.
Cover image © Bloomicon/Adobe Stock.

♾ This paper meets the requirements of ANSI/NISO Z39.48–1992 (Permanence of Paper).
Printed in the United States of America

28 27 26 25 24   5 4 3 2 1

CONTENTS

INTRODUCTION

FROM MAKERSPACES TO BOOK CLUBS, FROM MEDIA FACILITIES TO GROUP study spaces, from special events to book displays, libraries support learning in numerous ways. This book is intended to help librarians better understand how people learn so that they can improve support for learning on their campuses and in their communities.

This book reviews theories related to learning. But what is learning? Learning is not something that occurs only in classrooms or through *instruction*, which consists of a sequence of events designed to support learning.[1] Instead, people are learning constantly in a variety of settings. While learning is not synonymous with instruction, learning theories can and should inform the design of instruction. Throughout this book, the links between learning theories and instructional methods are explained in order to make these connections clear.

Learning has been defined in various ways. Many definitions of learning focus on the acquisition of knowledge and skills, but all definitions emphasize that learning results in change. Thus, *learning* can be defined more broadly as any change that occurs in skills, knowledge, attitudes, or values that is not due to the normal processes of biological growth. Furthermore, changes resulting from learning are somewhat lasting and are gained through experiences such as thinking, doing activities, or observing others.[2]

Theories provide a set of principles for explaining phenomena. While anyone can develop a theory based on their own guesses or intuitions, most theories that are widely accepted are based on an accumulation of evidence. Learning theories provide frameworks for organizing and understanding research findings related to learning, and they serve as the basis on which further research questions are developed for exploration. For the sake of conciseness, the vast quantities of research that support the development of learning theories have not been presented in this book; instead, the focus is on the major principles comprising the theories themselves.

Because learning encompasses a wide range of experiences, many different theories have been proposed to explain how people learn. The ideas behind the learning theories described in this book have come from the fields of psychology, education, philosophy, and anthropology, among others. Most of them were developed in the twentieth century, although they were influenced by centuries of ideas that came before. While behavioral learning theory dominated in the first half of the twentieth century, other theories rose to prominence in the century's second half, including constructivist theory, social cognitive theory, sociocultural theory, information processing theory, and self-regulation theory.[3]

No one theory is able to explain all learning. Different learning theories may be better or worse at explaining different kinds of learning for different individuals. Thus, theories can comfortably coexist, helping to explain diverse learning experiences or situations. While these theories are distinct, they also share many similarities. For example, many theories characterize learning as an active, complex process involving the interplay of thoughts, emotions, motivations, and social, environmental, and other factors. Thus, the theories described in this book are able to comfortably coexist with each other. In addition, the explanations provided here are intended to show how different concepts and theories relate to each other to form a more comprehensive picture of learning as a whole.

Many books on learning theory, typically written for students of education, are organized according to major theory, sometimes presented chronologically. This book, however, is organized into fourteen topics that are relevant to the work of librarians, with information about the relevant theories presented in each chapter as appropriate. This book can be read from cover to cover, or readers can jump around to the topics that interest them. Each chapter also contains parenthetical cross-references to indicate when related information is covered in a different chapter.

Several theories are applicable to multiple topics and are therefore addressed in multiple chapters. For instance, information processing theory is relevant to both focusing attention (chapter 3) and the ingestion of content through multimedia (chapter 4). Constructivist theory (chapter 1) is pertinent for learning through the process of collaboration (chapter 2), context (chapter 9), dialogue (chapter 10), inquiry (chapter 11), and imagination (chapter 12), so it reappears in several places.

The content in each chapter applies to a variety of library types and levels. While learning theories are the same no matter what level of learner is being engaged, they will, of course, be applied differently depending upon the circumstances. For example, the theories described in chapter 3, "Attention," are important for both younger and older learners, both of whom must direct their attention in order to be able to learn.

Each chapter follows a consistent format and includes the following sections:

- *Theoretical Overview:* This section begins each chapter and summarizes the most relevant aspects of theories and related instructional methods regarding each topic.
- *Implications for Libraries:* Because it can often be difficult to understand how to implement theoretical content, the practical guidance offered in this section shows how librarians can apply these theories to library spaces, services, resources, and technologies.
- *Teaching Librarian's Corner:* This section provides suggestions for how to apply theories to a range of instructional contexts, such as information literacy instruction and the teaching of maker or media skills.
- *Further Reading:* Recommended readings are included in this section.
- *Questions to Consider:* Reflection questions regarding the application of theory to library settings are provided in this section.

While librarians are constantly assisting learners, many may not be familiar with some of the theories that underlie educational and instructional practices or may not understand how these theories relate to their own work. Understanding learning theories may not only help librarians better plan for instruction, but it may also help them design services and spaces, provide rationales for funding requests, promote their contributions, and better assess what works. Hopefully, this book can help librarians achieve some of these goals.

ACKNOWLEDGMENTS

This work was completed with the support of a research sabbatical from the University of Nevada, Reno.

NOTES

1. Robert M. Gagné, Leslie J. Briggs, and Walter W. Wager, *Principles of Instructional Design*, 4th ed. (Fort Worth, TX: Harcourt Brace Jovanovich, 1992), 185.

2. Robert M. Gagné, *The Conditions of Learning*, 3rd ed. (New York: Holt, Rinehart and Winston, 1977), 3; Dale Schunk, *Learning Theories: An Educational Perspective*, 8th ed. (New York: Pearson, 2019), 3–4; Margaret E. Gredler, *Learning and Instruction: Theory into Practice*, 6th ed. (Upper Saddle River, NJ: Pearson, 2009), 145.

3. Thomas J. Shuell, "Theories of Learning," in *Psychology of Classroom Learning: An Encyclopedia*, ed. Eric M. Anderman and Lynley H. Anderman, vol. 2, 2 vols. (Detroit: Gale Cengage Learning, 2009), 935–39.

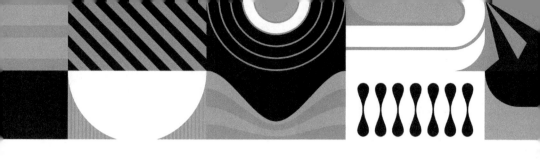

CONSTRUCTING KNOWLEDGE

THEORETICAL OVERVIEW

Are learners empty vessels, waiting to be filled with knowledge, preferably imparted by a wise teacher? Or are they more active participants in generating meaning and understanding? These questions are addressed by the theory of *constructivism*, which describes the ways that learners actively construct their own understandings when encountering new information.[1] Libraries have become essential in providing the resources, technologies, and tools that help learners to construct knowledge.

Constructivism is often opposed to another major learning theory that became prominent in the first half of the twentieth century: behaviorism. To understand the idea of constructing knowledge, it can be helpful to know more about the ways that constructivism differs from behaviorism, as well as the work of Jean Piaget and Lev Semyonovich Vygotsky, two theorists who had an enormous impact on the development of the idea of knowledge construction.

Constructivism vs. Behaviorism

Unlike constructivism, the theory of *behaviorism* describes how behaviors are learned in response to environmental cues. Behaviorism emphasizes the effects of external motivation and repeated practice in the learning of discrete skills and behaviors that can be observed and measured.[2] Behaviorists conceive of learning in terms of repeated responses to stimuli. These responses are learned through positive and negative reinforcement, which can be used to train learners to repeat or avoid certain behaviors. This repeated reinforcement supports the development of certain neural pathways in the brain. Behaviorism describes the mechanisms whereby behaviors are repeated over time until they are performed better and faster through continued reinforcement. For example, when teaching a dog to sit, an owner associates the sitting behavior with a particular cue (such as a hand signal or the word "sit") and teaches the dog to repeat that behavior through rewards (such as treats or praise). Over time, the dog performs the sitting behavior faster and more consistently.

The process of manipulating the environment to reinforce certain behaviors is called *conditioning*. Ivan Pavlov (1849–1936), a Russian physiologist, and B. F. Skinner (1904–1990), an American psychologist, were two of the first scientists to describe this process, which involves associating behaviors with particular environmental cues (e.g., a dog salivating whenever it hears the sound of a bell) and using punishments and rewards to reinforce and shape certain behaviors. While the experiments of the early behaviorists were initially performed with animals, the principles of behaviorism are widely applied in learning situations of all kinds whenever rewards or punishments (even those as simple as verbal praise or disapproval) provide reinforcement for or serve as inhibitors of certain behaviors.

In contrast to behaviorism, constructivism conceives of learning not as repeated behaviors in response to stimuli but as the mental construction of knowledge and skills that occurs within individuals when they encounter new information in their environment and reconcile it with their existing understanding. Constructivism, however, can be understood as a philosophical theory in addition to being a learning theory. As a philosophical theory, constructivism addresses *epistemology*—that is, the nature of knowledge and how people come to know about their world. From this perspective, constructivist theorists assert that people actively construct knowledge on the basis of their individual experiences and beliefs, many of which are culturally determined.[3] Thus, knowledge is thought to be inherently subjective and personal, and objective truth is either not possible or not knowable.

As a learning theory, constructivism describes how the process of knowing occurs within each person. Constructivist learning theorists maintain that knowledge is not necessarily a thing that individuals acquire but is instead constructed within the mind of each individual learner. In other words, knowledge is not simply imparted to another, but rather, learners construct their own understandings of the world by connecting new information with what they already know. Learning thus begins with each person's unique experiences and interests. Because any two people have different values and understandings, they may learn different knowledge and skills even when presented with the very same instruction. Knowledge, then, does not consist of objective truths about "real life" but of individual constructions that occur in relation to environmental stimuli.

Finally, constructivist learning theory is not so much a single theory as it is a theoretical family that provides the guiding principles upon which many other theories are based, including collaborative learning (described in chapter 2, "Collaboration"), situated learning (described in chapter 9, "Context"), inquiry-based learning (described in chapter 11, "Inquiry"), and many others.

Constructivist Learning Theory

While the theory behind constructivism was fully developed in recent times, its origins can be found in the work of several thinkers and philosophers, even those from thousands of years ago. In the time of ancient Greece, for example, Plato described how Socrates used questioning to help learners discover their own answers and arrive at their own understandings of complex ideas.

The thinker who has had perhaps the most important influence on modern notions of constructivist learning theory is Swiss psychologist Jean Piaget (1896–1980), who wrote hundreds of books and articles on child development and other topics, including philosophy, biology, and zoology. Piaget described four different stages that children pass through as they acquire knowledge and develop the ability to think at higher levels:

1. *Sensorimotor*, when young children use movement to respond to the world through their senses
2. *Preoperational*, when children begin to think symbolically (e.g., use language) and to create mental constructs and patterns to make sense of information received from their environment
3. *Concrete operational*, when children begin to use logical thinking about concrete events and to revise their previously formed mental constructs about the world
4. *Formal operational*, when adolescents or young adults begin to think abstractly, use deductive reasoning, apply abstract thinking to different situations, and continue to revise their previous mental constructs

Piaget's work on child development was instrumental in helping to explain how people process information that shapes their understanding.[4] Piaget argued that learners do not passively ingest information; rather, they actively structure and categorize information when adapting to environmental stimuli through the development of schemas. A *schema* is an individual's mental system for structuring and organizing information associated with concepts, ideas, or experiences. The process of learning occurs because people create their own mental structures or templates that help them process information that they receive from the world around them.[5] For example, public services librarians have schemas for navigating research and technology consultations that include a sequence of steps, expectations for interactions, common questions to ask, technologies to use, and so on. Schemas provide a framework for learning to occur because they enable new information to be more readily incorporated into existing understandings. Over time, a learner's schemas become more sophisticated through repeated exposure to new information. People with different types of intelligence, such as music, math, or visual intelligence (see chapter 14, "Individual Differences"), build different mental structures to shape their understandings of the world and then use those existing structures to create new structures.[6]

One of the central concepts of Piaget's theory revolves around the role that cognitive conflict plays in learning. *Cognitive conflict* occurs when learners encounter new information from their environment that conflicts with their current understandings. This old and new information presents an uncomfortable contradiction in the minds of learners, who long to resolve this conflict and achieve a harmonious mental state. Piaget referred to this harmonious mental state between a learner's internal cognitive structures and external information as *equilibration*.[7] To achieve equilibration when encountering new information, learners draw upon their existing knowledge, their prior experiences, and their cognitive skills in order to make sense of the new information and incorporate it into their thought processes.

Piaget described two processes through which learners make sense of new information received from their environment. With *assimilation*, learners incorporate new information from their environment into their existing schemas. Their existing mental structures are enhanced by this new information. With *accommodation*, learners change their existing schemas in order to make sense of the new information that they encounter in their environment. Learners must use accommodation to achieve a kind of mental balance when, for instance, things do not work as expected or when two different but valid arguments are presented to explain the same phenomenon or event. This process of reconciling conflicting information results in a mental reordering or reorganizing that leads to learning and cognitive growth.[8] Thus, assimilation and accommodation describe the ways that learners construct their own knowledge, as they process information from the environment in accordance with their own unique mental structures.

Piaget's theory of development suggests that learners are not "blank slates"; rather, learning is an active process on the part of the learner. In practice, this means that educators cannot simply deliver knowledge to learners but instead must help to facilitate learning by engaging learners in an active process that allows for the experience of cognitive conflict. Through the experience of cognitive conflict, learners transform concepts, construct their own understandings, and represent their learning in unique ways. Constructivist theory supports a role for educators that moves away from lectures, memorization, repetition, set curricula, the use of textbooks, "right" answers, and standardized tests. Instead, librarians and other educators should create learning situations that enable learners to experience the cognitive conflict that forces them to think through problems and contradictions in order to develop new understandings. They should attempt to facilitate and organize *active learning situations* that allow learners to become mentally engaged with the content, enabling them to take control of their own learning and to construct knowledge for themselves.

However, while learners may encounter new information that challenges their existing mental structures, this does not mean that they will necessarily change their thinking. Learners can simply ignore or reject the new information and persist in their current understandings. For librarians and other educators, this means that they should attempt to become aware of learners' stages of development and create learning situations that are appropriate. If educators present content that is beyond learners' abilities to process it, then learners will not be able to assimilate or accommodate it in a way that leads to growth.

Furthermore, a constructivist approach to instruction is not useful in all cases and for all content. Constructivist approaches that provide minimal guidance may fail novice learners who do not possess a sufficient collection of information and learning strategies to help them solve problems. For many types of learning situations, it is necessary to provide close instructional guidance, rather than unguided exploration and discovery.[9] To illustrate, it would be difficult for learners to arrive at their own understandings of certain math and science concepts, such as the rules for algebra or the theory of evolution.

Finally, librarians and other educators may need to intervene if they see that learners are going down the wrong path. During library instruction, for example, librarians should provide guidance if they observe that learners are making questionable judgments about the credibility and reliability of online sources, even if learners have constructed those ideas on their own. Thus, it is often necessary for librarians and other educators to integrate more guided, non-constructivist teaching strategies with constructivist approaches, depending on the content and skills being taught.

....

Assimilation and Accommodation during a Research Consultation

A librarian is helping a student who is researching the issue of gun control laws in the United States. The student is familiar with recent episodes of violence and understands that gun control legislation differs geographically because of the balance of power that exists between the federal and state governments. In the course of her research, the student learns new information about the Second Amendment of the U.S. Constitution, which allows citizens to possess firearms, as well as the history of some views of guns in different states. She *assimilates* this new information into her current understanding of gun control legislation at the state and federal levels. In addition, the student also learns about the efforts of special interest groups to influence gun control legislation. In doing so, she learns that these organizations play a significant role in the passage of legislation through lobbying, media campaigns, and voter mobilization—notions which challenge her current understanding of the ways that laws are passed and information is produced and shared. She *accommodates* this new information by changing her mental structures about both the workings of government and the production of information.

....

Social Constructivism

While constructivist learning theory describes how learners derive their own understandings, different perspectives on constructivism explain this notion in distinct ways. Are learners constructing new knowledge? Are they reconstructing existing knowledge? Or are they doing some combination thereof?

In addition to having different points of view regarding what is meant by knowledge construction, scholars of constructivist learning theory differ as to whether they believe that the source of learning exists within the learner, within the social environment, or through some interaction between the two. *Social constructivism*, a version of constructivist theory, maintains that knowledge is constructed through social interaction.[10]

The ideas behind this view of the role of the social in constructing meaning have been heavily influenced by the work of the Russian psychologist Lev Vygotsky[11] (further described in chapter 2, "Collaboration"; and chapter 13, "Guidance"). Vygotsky explained how knowledge is transmitted through cultural products such as language and mathematical symbols, which have been developed through social interaction. He described how the social environment influences thinking, as people internalize speech to help them regulate their own thought processes in response to information received from the environment. Moreover, dialogue with others leads to cognitive development and the creation of shared meanings. Thus, language not only represents previously constructed meanings but is used to construct meanings too.

According to social constructivist thought, social context is important for learning in different ways. People learn through communication with others that occurs in social settings, and social interaction shapes the manner in which learning occurs. Discussion with others provides a means through which knowledge is shared and learners shape and develop their own ideas. When they are not learning through person-to-person communication, they often learn through information contained in products created by others, such as written information and visual media. Furthermore, knowledge itself is created by human beings who participate in meaning-making activities within cultural contexts. From this perspective, knowledge is a product of shared social activities, and learning occurs as a result of participation in cultural practices. Knowledge structures evolve over time through social interaction and are shared through cultural dissemination.[12]

Those who espouse constructivist theory differ as to how they construe the prominence of social interaction in learning. "Cognitive constructivists" assert that knowledge construction is a process that occurs solely within individuals, while "social constructivists" contend that knowledge construction occurs through interaction between the individual and the social. For cognitive constructivists, learning occurs through the individual process of reorganizing thought in response to cognitive conflict. For social constructivists, learning is a process that occurs through participation in cultural practices.[13]

While these two views may seem like they are at odds with each other, both approaches provide valuable insights into how learning occurs and how instructional situations can be designed to enhance learning. Both approaches to constructivist theory suggest that learners must be actively engaged in the process. Thus, librarians and other educators should strive to create instructional situations that allow learners to execute tasks and interact with content in such a way that they can discover knowledge for themselves.

IMPLICATIONS FOR LIBRARIES

While the process of constructing knowledge is an internal one, it is often external activity that provides the source of the cognitive conflict that serves as an impetus for learning, and thus, constructivist learning frequently involves learning activities. In addition, constructivist learning often involves social interaction, in which learners can come together and share their ideas with each other. A constructivist approach to instruction encourages learners to generate their own questions, dig deep for their own answers, and demonstrate their own learning. Finally, constructivism also supports an interdisciplinary approach to learning content that focuses on big ideas that are broadly applicable, conceptual understandings that make connections across boundaries, and open-ended problems that require the use of different approaches when generating solutions. Libraries can provide spaces, resources, and opportunities that support these types of engagement.

Librarians can use some of the following strategies to support constructivist approaches to learning:

- Work with educators to purchase materials that can supplement or replace traditional textbooks and allow learners to connect with material in different ways.
- Promote the use of physical and digital primary sources as a means for learners to engage with original material, generate their own questions, and develop their own perspectives.
- Provide various types of group spaces that allow learners to engage in dialogue and discussion.
- Provide physical and online forums in which people from different disciplines can come together to exchange ideas.
- Host speakers who present challenging ideas from a variety of perspectives and include time for attendees to respond with ideas of their own.
- Lend tools and technologies that allow learners to make or design things, such as cameras, electronics, robotics equipment, anatomical models, building toys, sewing supplies, and bird-watching kits.
- Lead citizen science (www.citizenscience.gov) or nature education programs and projects that allow for hands-on learning. Partner with community organizations to bring hands-on learning experiences into the library or bring library patrons into the community.
- Provide physical and digital forums that present the products of learning, such as displays where learners can show their designs or models, spaces where learners can give public presentations, or web pages where learners can share their writing or artwork.

TEACHING LIBRARIAN'S CORNER

During instructional situations, librarians can integrate constructivist learning theory by attempting to grasp learners' current understandings and interests, and then adjust their instruction accordingly. Librarians should help learners to engage with issues and problems that challenge their understandings, connect to big ideas, pursue issues of interest to them, generate their own questions, and seek their own answers. Librarians can work with other educators to create learning situations that allow learners to discover resources, collect and analyze their own data for research projects, and present the results of their inquiries. They can introduce opportunities that allow learners to touch, manipulate, design, and make objects. Finally, they can partner with community groups to bring learning into real-world settings that provide learners with opportunities to generate their own questions.

Librarians can use some of the following strategies to incorporate constructivist theory into instruction:

- Activate learners' prior knowledge of a topic by asking them to review or reflect upon what they already know about it.
- Ask learners to share their understanding of concepts before provid-ing "official" definitions or lists (e.g., ask learners to define the term "research" or generate their own criteria for evaluating information sources).
- Encourage learners to pursue their own interests or choose their own topics for exploration.
- Teach learners to use reference works as a way to gain background infor-mation about new topics to help them construct schemas that can aid in processing information from more advanced and in-depth sources.
- Provide opportunities for learners to use primary sources and data to generate their own ideas and interpretations about the factors sur-rounding current and historical events.
- Ask learners to investigate various perspectives on complex problems and contemporary issues. For example, learners can summarize and respond to ideas from sources that present conflicting ideas.
- Ask open-ended questions designed to challenge beliefs and current understandings. Encourage learners to engage in dialogue that enables them to share their perspectives, justify their ideas to others, and chal-lenge each other's opinions.

- Let learners make errors (e.g., when searching for information or when designing an object in a library makerspace), give helpful hints to get them on the right track, and encourage them to learn from their mistakes.
- Encourage learners to reflect upon what they have learned either in writing or orally (e.g., reflect upon their information search processes or reflect upon which parts of an assignment were the most challenging). Use learners' reflections to gauge their thinking, address big ideas and concepts, and provide guidance when concepts are poorly or partially understood.
- Encourage learners to share what they know through the creation of products or presentations that allow them to explain what they are thinking. Provide learners with some choice about how they want to represent their own learning (e.g., create a poster, construct a book, make an object, design a plan or program, etc.).

....

Using Primary Sources for Constructivist Learning

Using primary sources provides an excellent opportunity for employing a constructivist approach to learning. Primary sources can give learners room to analyze events themselves, evaluate decisions, draw comparisons, experiment with ideas, and come to their own conclusions. For instance, if learners are studying early twentieth-century American vaudeville performances, they can use primary-source video, audio, images, and reviews from that time period. When used in combination with secondary sources, primary sources can help learners to explore and arrive at their own interpretations about the reasons for vaudeville's popularity, its reflections of society and culture, its depictions of race and gender, the reasons for its eventual decline, and its influence on contemporary performance styles. Learners could even use their new understandings of this performance genre to construct their own entertainments in a similar style.

....

FURTHER READING

Brooks, Jacqueline Grennon, and Martin G. Brooks. *In Search of Understanding: The Case for Constructivist Classrooms.* Alexandria, VA: Association for Supervision & Curriculum Development, 1999.

Fosnot, Catherine T., ed. *Constructivism: Theory, Perspectives, and Practice.* 2nd ed. New York: Teachers College Press, 2005.

Pritchard, Alan, and John Woollard. *Psychology for the Classroom: Constructivism and Social Learning.* New York: Taylor & Francis Group, 2010.

QUESTIONS TO CONSIDER

1. What is cognitive conflict? What are some strategies that librarians can use to ensure that learners experience cognitive conflict during library instruction or events?

2. Describe a variety of activities or events that you could hold in a library of your choosing that promote a constructivist approach to learning.

3. For what kinds of library instruction situations would a constructivist approach to instruction be appropriate? For what kinds of situations would it be inappropriate?

NOTES

1. Catherine Twomey Fosnot and Randall Stewart Perry, "Constructivism: A Psychological Theory of Learning," in *Constructivism: Theory, Perspectives, and Practice*, ed. Catherine Twomey Fosnot, 2nd ed. (New York: Teachers College Press, 2005), 8–38; David William Jardine, *Piaget & Education: Primer* (New York: Lang, 2006), 21; Alan Pritchard, *Ways of Learning: Learning Theories and Learning Styles in the Classroom*, 3rd ed. (London: Routledge, 2014), 18.

2. Pritchard, *Ways of Learning*, 6–17.

3. Alan Pritchard and John Woollard, *Psychology for the Classroom: Constructivism and Social Learning* (New York: Taylor & Francis Group, 2010), 2–4.

4. Jardine, *Piaget & Education*, 17–51; Fosnot and Perry, "Constructivism: A Psychological Theory of Learning"; Jean Piaget, "Piaget's Theory," in *Piaget and His School: A Reader in Developmental Psychology*, ed. Bärbel Inhelder, Harold H. Chipman, and Charles Zwingmann (New York: Springer-Verlag, 1976), 11–23; Jean Piaget, *The Equilibration of Cognitive Structures: The Central Problem of Intellectual Development*, trans. Terrance Brown and Kishore Julian Thampy (Chicago: University of Chicago Press, 1985).

5. Pritchard, *Ways of Learning*, 22–25; Jardine, *Piaget & Education*, 6.

6. Fosnot and Perry, "Constructivism: A Psychological Theory of Learning."

7. Piaget, *The Equilibration of Cognitive Structures*; Jean Piaget, "Problems of Equilibration," in *The Essential Piaget*, ed. Howard E. Gruber and J. Jacques Voneche (New York: Basic Books, 1977), 838–41; Jean Piaget, "Equilibration Processes in the Psychobiological Development of the Child," in *The Essential Piaget*, ed. Howard E. Gruber and J. Jacques Voneche (New York: Basic Books, 1977), 832–37; Piaget, "Piaget's Theory."

8. Piaget, "Piaget's Theory"; Piaget, *The Equilibration of Cognitive Structures*, 3–35; Piaget, "Problems of Equilibration"; Piaget, "Equilibration Processes in the Psychobiological Development of the Child."

9. Paul A. Kirschner, John Sweller, and Richard E. Clark, "Why Minimal Guidance during Instruction Does Not Work: An Analysis of the Failure of Constructivist, Discovery, Problem-Based, Experiential, and Inquiry-Based Teaching," *Educational Psychologist* 41, no. 2 (June 1, 2006): 75–86, https://doi.org/10.1207/s15326985ep4102_1.

10. Elizabeth F. Barkley, Claire Howell Major, and K. Patricia Cross, *Collaborative Learning Techniques: A Handbook for College Faculty*, 2nd ed., Jossey-Bass Higher and Adult Education Series (San Francisco: Jossey-Bass, 2013), 9, 17; Angela M. O'Donnell and Cindy E. Hmelo-Silver, "Introduction: What Is Collaborative Learning? An Overview," in *The International Handbook of Collaborative Learning*, ed. Cindy E. Hmelo-Silver et al. (New York: Routledge, 2013), 1–15; Pritchard, *Ways of Learning*, 6–9, 34–38.

11. L. S. Vygotsky, *Mind in Society: The Development of Higher Psychological Processes*, ed. Michael Cole (Cambridge, MA: Harvard University Press, 1978); Fosnot and Perry, "Constructivism: A Psychological Theory of Learning."

12. Cynthia M. D'Angelo, Stephanie Touchman, and Douglas B. Clark, "Constructivism: Overview," in *Psychology of Classroom Learning: An Encyclopedia*, ed. Eric M. Anderman and Lynley H. Anderman, vol. 1, 2 vols. (Detroit: Gale Cengage Learning, 2009), 262–67.

13. Paul Cobb, "Where Is the Mind? A Coordination of Sociocultural and Cognitive Constructivist Perspectives," in *Constructivism: Theory, Perspectives, and Practice*, ed. Catherine Twomey Fosnot, 2nd ed. (New York: Teachers College Press, 2005), 39–57.

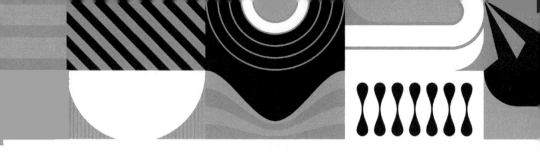

2

COLLABORATION

THEORETICAL OVERVIEW

Collaborative learning, or group work as it is commonly called, has become increasingly common over the last few decades and is now used for instruction across almost all grade levels and disciplines. *Collaborative learning* refers to the use of small groups of students to achieve common learning outcomes in intentionally structured learning situations.[1] Libraries play an important role in supporting collaborative learning by providing spaces and opportunities that enable learners to interact with each other.

Approaches to instruction that use collaborative learning have been heavily influenced not only by sociocultural learning theory and the work of Vygotsky, but also by several other theoretical approaches.

Sociocultural Theory

Lev Semyonovich Vygotsky (1896–1934) was a Russian psychologist and educator who wrote in the years following the Russian Revolution of 1917. He was influenced by the writings of Karl Marx, whose ideas about social change and its impact on the individual are prominent in Vygotsky's writings about learning.[2]

Vygotsky and other theorists have contributed to the *sociocultural theory* of development (also called social historical theory), which describes how individuals' cognitive development relates to cultural, historical, and institutional contexts.[3] At the very center of learning is *culture*, which is the learned behavior of a group of people that is passed down through generations.[4] Vygotsky located learning within the social activity of a culture that is continually evolving. Just as culture is influenced by the individuals that comprise it, an individual's thinking is closely related to the cultural context in which that person matures. Vygotsky was one of the first scholars to fully articulate the implications of this idea. In addition to influencing the development of sociocultural theory, his description of the ways that social interaction forms the basis for thinking and learning also influenced the version of constructivist theory known as social constructivism (described in chapter 1, "Constructing Knowledge").

Through its forms and structures, culture influences both what is learned and how that learning occurs. Through shared activities and relationships, humans imbue objects and sounds with cultural meaning. Just as humans have developed physical tools that allow them to master their environment, they have developed psychological tools as well. These *psychological tools* consist of cultural constructs such as writing, numbers, and drawing. Children learn the shared psychological tools of their culture, and their meanings are passed down from one generation to the next. These psychological tools are not only important for communicating within a particular culture, but they also play a much more fundamental role in human development. In fact, they serve to structure thinking itself. They shape the ways that thinking develops within individuals and the ability of learners to think at higher levels.

Vygotsky described two separate but interrelated processes of cognitive development: learning these psychological tools, such as language and counting, and employing these tools in the execution of higher-level cognitive tasks, such as analysis and problem-solving. According to Vygotsky, a child first learns to make meaning through interactions with others using psychological tools. The child then internalizes these tools to structure their own thought processes. Vygotsky described this process as follows:

> An interpersonal process is transformed into an intrapersonal one. Every function in the child's cultural development appears twice: first, on the social level, and later, on the individual level: first, between people (interpsychological), and then inside the child (intrapsychological). . . . All the higher functions originate as actual relations between human individuals.[5]

While learning occurs differently for each individual, Vygotsky conceptualized thinking as an inherently shared process, and he identified social interaction as the basis for learning. Individual cognitive development originates in the social world before becoming internalized. In other words, higher-level cognitive development comes after social interaction.

Speech is one type of psychological tool that not only serves as a means of communication but also affects the very process of thinking. At young ages, children learn to communicate through speech. As they mature, they internalize speech, which then serves as a tool that they use to regulate their behavior and structure their thinking, thereby impacting their higher-level cognitive processes.

People's thought processes are not only affected by social and cultural experiences, but they are also partially determined by them. The example of speech described above demonstrates how all cultural tools not only shape thought, but potentially limit it as well. To illustrate, the types of vocabulary available through a particular language influence a learner's ability not just to describe their surroundings but also to conceptualize the opportunities and challenges that they encounter within their environments.

Because each culture develops its own unique psychological tools, the way that thinking develops in individuals will inevitably be determined by the culture in which one lives and the institutions of that culture. For learners, this means that thinking will be influenced not just by the subject they are learning and the texts they are reading, but by the cultural institutions of schools and libraries in which that learning occurs.[6] For a learner who attends a school or visits a library, the cultural context includes the arrangement of the classroom and library spaces, and the items within those spaces, such as posters on the wall and books on the shelves, all of which influence what and how a person learns.

Collaborative Learning

Collaborative learning theory supports the notion that learning is enhanced through personal interactions. This can be seen in the role of peer discussion in effecting the cognitive conflict that leads to learning, an aspect of constructivist theory (see chapter 1, "Constructing Knowledge"). Cognitive conflict occurs when learners encounter new information that conflicts with their current understandings and must work to resolve the conflicting information. While Jean Piaget, who elaborated on this concept, believed that knowledge construction occurs within the individual, he also recognized that social interaction can play a role in the resolution of cognitive conflict.[7] This occurs when learners discuss a topic and challenge each other's perspectives. For example, when two learners discuss information related to a controversy and present different points of view about it, each will experience some cognitive conflict that they must then reconcile by reflecting on what they hear and working through its potential implications for their ideas. While learning can result from discussion among any individuals, Piaget described how peer discussions are especially well-suited for enabling learning to occur.[8] Because of their unequal status, children might be more likely to accept what adults say without question, which may prevent them from experiencing cognitive conflict. However, because of the equal power relations that exist among peers, they may be more likely to challenge each other's ideas during discussions, leading to the kind of cognitive restructuring that results in learning.

Information processing theory (described in chapter 3, "Attention") also provides some insight into the cognitive mechanisms that occur on an interpersonal level during collaborative learning. Information processing theory describes the ways that information is processed and stored in memory. Collaborative learning scenarios are designed to actively engage learners by using social interaction to help them connect pieces of information and organize them into meaningful concepts to facilitate further mental processing. The communication processes of speaking and listening during group work can assist with this processing function. Once information has been ingested, it must be rehearsed and restructured for it to be retained in memory, and the process of explaining concepts to other learners in collaborative learning situations can aid retention.[9] The act of listening to the explanations of others also helps with cognitive processing as learners compare new information with prior understandings, recognize contradictions, create connections among ideas, and prepare to respond to other learners. As group members challenge each other's ideas, learners must examine their prior knowledge, assess inaccuracies, and use incoming information to develop new models of understanding.[10]

Collaborative learning theory also asserts that community is essential to learning, an idea that has been strongly influenced by sociocultural theory. Communities are formed when people with different perspectives come together and negotiate shared understandings. This concept of community extends to the classroom, where learners from different backgrounds bring their own understandings to the formation of a classroom community. Kenneth Bruffee, a scholar of collaborative learning, has explained that knowledge is derived through communicating with others in a process of negotiation and consensus-building within a community.[11] From this perspective, the teacher is not the ultimate source of knowledge and authority in the classroom; rather, the teacher becomes part of a knowledge community in collaboration with the students.

Collaborative learning pedagogy reinforces the concept that knowledge is not a thing to be acquired but is instead a product of a community of knowledgeable peers that is represented in the language of that community. Collaborative learning models the process of knowledge generation and sharing, thereby preparing learners to participate in the many knowledge communities with which they will engage in the future.[12] Because collaboration does not always come naturally, people need to learn how to share their thoughts and beliefs in such a way that they become valuable members of the groups that they will join throughout the course of their lives.

Librarians and other educators can support collaborative learning by creating intentionally structured learning activities that involve peer interaction, dialogue, cooperation, and collaboration. However, while many learners enjoy learning collaboratively, it is not uncommon for an announcement of a group activity to be greeted with groans. While some learners are eager to do well on a group activity, others put forth as little effort as possible. To address these potential problems, David W. Johnson and Roger T. Johnson, two scholars of a version of collaborative learning known as "cooperative learning," theorized about the characteristics of successful group learning:

- *Positive interdependence:* The success of each group member is dependent on the whole, and all group members are united in a common effort toward a joint goal, often with shared rewards.
- *Individual accountability:* Each group member is held accountable for completing their share of the work, thus ensuring that no one member is free riding.
- *Promotive interaction:* Group members help each other to succeed by providing support, assistance, encouragement, and explanation.
- *Social skills:* Group members use communication, trust-building, leadership, decision-making, and conflict-management skills to ensure the success of the whole.
- *Group processing:* Group members use discussion to assess their progress toward achieving their goals and how they are functioning as a group.[13]

These five characteristics of successful groups suggest that librarians and other educators need to provide learners with considerable guidance in how to hold high-quality discourse and interactions that lead to learning. If they neglect to do this, groups may resort to working at the most basic level.

Information Literacy and the Influence of the Social

The influence of social-cultural and social constructivist theories of learning can be seen in recent conceptions of information literacy, which portray it as a collective practice that occurs within specific social contexts.[14] In fact, the Association of College and Research Libraries's *Framework for Information Literacy for Higher Education* recognizes the importance of the communal and contextual value of information in its various frames, such as "Scholarship as Conversation" and "Authority Is Constructed and Contextual." This can also be seen in its definition of information literacy as "the set of integrated abilities encompassing the reflective discovery of information, the understanding of how information is produced and valued, and the use of information in creating new knowledge and participating ethically in communities of learning."[15]

IMPLICATIONS FOR LIBRARIES

Because all collaborative learning is dependent on the processes of speaking and listening that form the basis of discussion and interaction, an essential requirement for group learning is having a place where learners can talk without disturbing others. In addition to providing spaces for collaboration, libraries can also provide technologies that support interactive projects, such as specialized software that groups need, wireless access to facilitate group use of technology, and shared monitors for group viewing. Because various groups have different needs, libraries should contain spaces that vary considerably, from large to small, from private rooms to open spaces, from rooms requiring reservation to first-come, first-served arrangements.

Here are a variety of strategies that librarians can use to support collaborative learning:

- Provide a variety of group study spaces, including private, semi-private, and open spaces. Publicize group spaces in libraries through the library website and maps. Enable learners to reserve group spaces in advance, and provide on-the-spot information about group spaces that are available for use.
- Provide spaces that support collaboration such as makerspaces, media labs, cafes, and *active learning classrooms* (i.e., learning spaces containing small group configurations and access to technology such as video screens for group viewing).
- Design library spaces with moveable furniture so that groups can configure spaces to their needs. Assist learners in configuring furniture and technologies for their needs.

- Provide whiteboards, whiteboard markers, shared monitors, and other tools that support group work in different library spaces.
- Provide signage or information on library websites about scheduled group meetings to allow learners to find their spaces and groups. Provide information that allows learners to locate like-minded people in the library with whom they can connect.
- Offer research or technology consultations to small groups of learners who are working on group projects. Offer instruction in how to use technologies that support collaborative learning.
- Provide research and technology support for educators who assign group work in online classes.
- Provide technologies, such as laptops or media equipment, that learners can check out to complete group projects.
- Host in-person events or online forums that enable groups to share the products of their collaborative learning efforts.

TEACHING LIBRARIAN'S CORNER

When implementing collaborative learning activities into their teaching, librarians can use a variety of approaches. Learners can be assigned to a group for a matter of minutes or for a whole semester. A group may consist of only two learners or many more. Group work may be completed in person or online. There is no one correct way to assign group work, and the way that group work is implemented varies greatly with the type and nature of an activity.

While the ideal size of a group depends on its purpose, groups become more difficult to manage the larger they get. Larger and more heterogeneous groups offer the possibility of hearing a range of perspectives. However, with more people comes a greater possibility for disagreement, difficulty in working toward a common goal, and difficulty with equalizing participation. Furthermore, in larger groups, some quieter learners will refrain from speaking up, even if they have ideas to contribute.

Librarians can use some of the following strategies to incorporate collaborative learning in instruction:

- Use group discussion in situations in which learners would benefit from exposure to multiple perspectives (e.g., discussing issues related to source evaluation, the assessment of evidence, the effects of the spread of false information, the determination of fair use, or the benefits and drawbacks of peer review).

- Implement structural supports for group work, such as providing clear directions for group tasks, assigning certain roles within groups, and demonstrating how groups can use certain technologies for group work. Establish clear evaluation criteria for group work.
- Teach learners strategies for asking complex questions in groups or for working together to analyze information critically, so that they do not work at too simple a level.
- Foster open, honest, and respectful communication by teaching strategies to help learners effectively handle disagreement (e.g., encourage learners to focus on ideas rather than the people expressing them, to avoid passing judgment, and to ask questions to try to understand underlying issues and perspectives).
- Check in frequently with groups and use multiple points of feedback to monitor group work and ensure that groups are working productively.
- Implement group reflections and assessments to ensure both individual and group accountability.
- Use discussion boards and other collaborative tools in learning management systems to add collaborative components to online learning situations.
- When creating instructional videos or online tutorials, appeal to learners' motivations to learn in a social context by using a conversational style, polite language, human (rather than machine) voices, and characters who use human gestures and movements.[16]

FURTHER READING

Barkley, Elizabeth F., Claire Howell Major, and K. Patricia Cross. *Collaborative Learning Techniques: A Handbook for College Faculty*. 2nd ed. San Francisco: Jossey-Bass, 2013.

O'Donnell, Angela M., and Cindy E. Hmelo-Silver, eds. *The International Handbook of Collaborative Learning*. New York: Routledge, 2013.

Vygotsky, L. S. *Mind in Society: The Development of Higher Psychological Processes*. Edited by Michael Cole. Cambridge, MA: Harvard University Press, 1978.

QUESTIONS TO CONSIDER

1. In what ways are culture and community linked to what people know and how they come to know it? What does this mean for education in general and libraries in particular?

2. Consider the varied types of spaces present in a library of your choosing. How has the design of those spaces been influenced (or not) by some of the ideas from collaborative learning theory?

3. What are some assessment strategies that can be used to determine whether collaboration spaces in libraries support learning?

NOTES

1. Elizabeth F. Barkley, Claire Howell Major, and K. Patricia Cross, *Collaborative Learning Techniques: A Handbook for College Faculty*, 2nd ed., Jossey-Bass Higher and Adult Education Series (San Francisco: Jossey-Bass, 2013), 4.

2. Michael Cole and Sylvia Scribner, "Introduction," in *Mind in Society: The Development of Higher Psychological Processes*, by L. S. Vygotsky, ed. Michael Cole et al. (Cambridge, MA: Harvard University Press, 1978), 1–16.

3. L. S. Vygotsky, *Mind in Society: The Development of Higher Psychological Processes*, ed. Michael Cole et al. (Cambridge, MA: Harvard University Press, 1978); National Academies of Sciences, Engineering, *How People Learn II: Learners, Contexts, and Cultures*, 2018, 26, https://doi.org/10.17226/24783; Barbara Rogoff, "Cognition as a Collaborative Process," in *Handbook of Child Psychology: Cognition, Perception, and Language*, ed. D. Kuhn and R. S. Siegler, vol. 2, 4 vols. (New York: Wiley, 1998), 679–744.

4. National Academies of Sciences, *How People Learn II*, 22.

5. Vygotsky, *Mind in Society*, 57.

6. Jonathan R. H. Tudge and Paul A. Winterhoff, "Vygotsky, Piaget, and Bandura: Perspectives on the Relations between the Social World and Cognitive Development," *Human Development* 36, no. 2 (1993): 61–81.

7. Rogoff, "Cognition as a Collaborative Process."

8. Angela M. O'Donnell and Cindy E. Hmelo-Silver, "Introduction: What Is Collaborative Learning? An Overview," in *The International Handbook of Collaborative Learning*, ed. Cindy E. Hmelo-Silver et al. (New York: Routledge, 2013), 1–15.

9. Noreen M. Webb, "Information Processing Approaches to Collaborative Learning," in *The International Handbook of Collaborative Learning*, ed. Cindy E. Hmelo-Silver et al. (New York: Routledge, 2013), 19–40; David W. Johnson and Roger T. Johnson, "Learning Groups," in *The Handbook of Group Research and Practice*, ed. Susan A. Wheelan (Thousand Oaks, CA: Sage, 2005), 441–61.

10. Webb, "Information Processing Approaches to Collaborative Learning."

11. Kenneth A. Bruffee, "Collaborative Learning and the 'Conversation of Mankind,'" in *Collaborative Learning: A Sourcebook for Higher Education*, ed. Anne Goodsell, Michelle Maher, and Vincent Tinto, vol. 1 (University Park, PA: National Center on Postsecondary Teaching, 1992), 23–33; Kenneth A. Bruffee, *Collaborative Learning: Higher Education, Interdependence, and the Authority of Knowledge*, 2nd ed. (Baltimore, MD: Johns Hopkins University Press, 1999).

12. Bruffee, "Collaborative Learning and the 'Conversation of Mankind,'" 30.

13. Johnson and Johnson, "Learning Groups."

14. Annemaree Lloyd, "Information Literacy as a Socially Enacted Practice: Sensitising Themes for an Emerging Perspective of People-in-Practice," *Journal of Documentation* 68, no. 6 (January 1, 2012): 772–83, https://doi.org/10.1108/00220411211277037.

15. Association of College & Research Libraries, "Framework for Information Literacy for Higher Education," 2016, www.ala.org/acrl/standards/ilframework.

16. Richard E. Mayer, *Multimedia Learning*, 3rd ed. (Cambridge: Cambridge University Press, 2020), 305–56.

3

ATTENTION

THEORETICAL OVERVIEW

Learners are surrounded by an overabundance of information that often makes it difficult to focus. But being able to direct one's attention is essential for learning. Because the demands of modern life and the proliferation of technologies create innumerable distractions, learners often turn to libraries to help them control their attention.

Attention, or the "mental energy used to perceive, think, and understand,"[1] consists of a set of cognitive abilities that allow learners to focus on cognitive or sensory information in order to accomplish tasks. If a learner does not focus their attention on what they are reading in a book or hearing from a teacher, then they will be unable to process and understand this information.

Current understandings of the role of attention have been influenced by models of information processing, which were first developed by cognitive scientists in the 1950s. Information processing models have subsequently influenced approaches to the design of instructional content as well as understandings of the role of attention in the digital age.

Information Processing

Attention is a critical component of the information processing theory of learning. *Information processing* describes a collection of models that concern the cognitive processes of receiving information, coding it in memory, and retrieving it for later use. Many of these models describe the ways that humans receive information from their environment through their senses, transfer that information to their working memory, and then rehearse that information for transference to their long-term memory.

Information processing models generally include three major components: sensory memory, working memory, and long-term memory (see figure 3.1). *Sensory memory* refers to the function of receiving incoming sensory stimuli and screening that information to determine whether it is relevant. Sensory information is received through the appropriate channel such as sight, sound, and smell and is processed as electrical impulses in the brain. Thousands of pieces of sensory information are absorbed each second, so the brain's sensory register filters out irrelevant information. It identifies relevant information and holds it for a few seconds in sensory memory so that it can be further processed in working memory.[2] Sensory memory can be activated through a conscious process of attending to certain stimuli but often occurs unconsciously, influenced by factors such as past experiences, assessment of threat levels, and emotional states, all of which can help or hinder the receipt of sensory information.[3]

Sensory information that is attended to is transferred into *working memory*, which refers to a short-term memory system in which information is processed. These processes involve activities that construct meaning, such as reflecting, examining, evaluating, integrating, and planning. The process of learning is concerned with these working memory functions. Working memory is governed by an *executive control system* that selects information for processing, selects strategies to use for processing, and uses auditory or visual-spatial subsystems for processing different kinds of information.[4] If the information in working memory is not reviewed and repeated, then it will soon be forgotten.

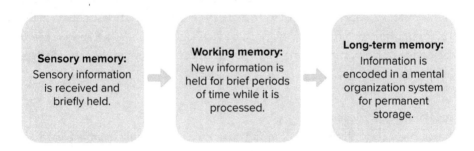

FIGURE 3.1

The three major components of information processing models

In order to process information in working memory, it must be continually attended to. However, some aspects of information processing require very little attention, while more challenging aspects, such as completing a calculus problem or reading dense passages of text, may require more attention. In addition, the storage capacity of working memory is limited. Adolescents and adults can process no more than a few pieces of information at a time. However, people can increase their working memory capacity by grouping, or *chunking*, several pieces of information into a single element.[5] Psychologist George Miller first described how people can hold about seven chunks of information in working memory at a time, although they can increase the size of those chunks to process more information.[6] Moreover, the length of time that a person can attend to and process new information in working memory varies greatly with age, ability, and level of motivation. Adolescents and adults can process new information for about 10–20 minutes at a time before needing to take a mental break or change the manner in which they are interacting with the information.[7]

If information in working memory is deemed important enough, then it is encoded in *long-term memory*, which refers to the brain's long-term storage system. The process of encoding involves mentally organizing and connecting new pieces of information with old ones. People are more likely to code information in long-term memory if it affects their survival, if they associate strong emotions with the information, if they can understand and make sense of the information, or if the information is relevant to their lives.[8]

Although the processing of information from the senses into long-term memory may appear to be composed of discrete, linear steps, it is actually quite dynamic, with many activities related to processing, remembering, retrieving, and forgetting occurring simultaneously. Moreover, the process need not begin with information from the senses; instead, information from long-term memory can provide the stimulus for information ingestion that then proceeds through processing in sensory and working memory.

Focus and Technology

Attention is influenced by several different areas in the brain, including the frontal lobes, which are responsible for higher-level thinking, and the limbic system, which is responsible for emotional reactions. The frontal lobes play an important role in selecting what to attend to, shifting attention among stimuli, and sustaining focus on complex topics. Attention is also strongly influenced by emotion. Attention plays a critical role in survival, as people must attend to stimuli that either enhance their well-being, leading to the experience of positive emotions (e.g., excitement at the smell of a delicious meal), or pose a threat, leading to the experience of negative emotions (e.g., fear at the sight of an approaching bear). Because of the role that emotions play in focusing attention, librarians and other educators often strive to maintain a safe atmosphere in the learning environment so that learners do not become distracted by negative emotions such as fear of being embarrassed in front of peers.

Attending to information involves the process of shifting focus from one stimulus to another and maintaining focus on the new stimulus. It therefore has several characteristics:

- *Orienting attention* describes the ability to move one's focus among different stimuli. When responding to stimuli in the environment, this often occurs through looking at the object of attention.
- *Sustaining attention* describes the ability to maintain focus on particular tasks. This is often demonstrated by being responsive to changes in the object of attention.
- *Divided attention* describes the ability to perform certain tasks simultaneously, often using different senses to process the information (such as driving while listening to music). Because mental processing power is limited, attention can be divided only among certain types of tasks before being compromised. The types of tasks that can be performed successfully with divided attention often use different skills (such as motor skills and cognitive skills).[9]

Because learners can pay attention to only a certain number of things at a time, they must be selective about what they direct their attention to and avoid dividing their limited attentional resources among multiple things (e.g., studying while watching a movie). With experience, learners can accomplish some types of cognitive activities automatically (such as adding or spelling), which allows them to perform those activities while simultaneously devoting their attention to tasks that are more cognitively demanding (such as solving a problem involving differential equations or writing an essay about a Shakespearean play).

The advent of new technologies, including the internet, has made it increasingly difficult for learners to focus their attention, a phenomenon that has implications for librarians who are helping learners use internet resources. This phenomenon has resulted from a number of factors, including the internet's constant interactivity, its use of links, its easy searchability, its social context, and its use of multimedia to convey messages.[10] The convergence of all of these factors often leads learners to have a highly fragmented experience when they interact with web content. For instance, when learners look at a web page, they are often overwhelmed with competing visual, textual, and auditory stimuli that can make it difficult to focus (discussed in chapter 4, "Multimedia"). The searchability of the web and the proliferation of links make it easy to rapidly alternate among pages without paying close attention to any one page in particular. When learners do find a page of interest, they often jump to the exact phrases or images that capture their attention rather than reading the entire content of the page in a linear fashion. Web interactions that occur on social networking sites also involve negotiating social status with others, which makes learners susceptible to emotions such as embarrassment, thereby deepening their involvement while making it more difficult to notice other stimuli. Thus, while the internet may capture learners' attention, it also may make it difficult for them to focus on complex information for sustained periods of time.[11]

While it is a common belief that technological devices allow learners to *multitask*, or pay attention to multiple things at once, it is virtually impossible to focus attention on two different cognitive tasks at the same time. Instead, what usually happens when learners attempt to multitask is that they move their attention back and forth between single tasks. This act of continually shifting among different tasks slows their ability to work effectively because their brains use additional processing power to adjust to the different goals and parameters associated with each activity.[12]

Technological devices also manipulate learners' attention in different ways. For example, learners may be instantly notified through a sound or visual cue when they receive a new e-mail or social media message, prompting them to interrupt whatever it is they are doing to interact with the new message. In fact, because technologies are constantly posing distractions, learners who use them are continually engaged in task-switching. The overwhelming demands on a learner's attention can lead to an increasing inability to focus. At extreme levels, this can even be characterized by feelings of distraction, loss of control, panic, dissatisfaction, guilt, impatience, stress, and being rushed and overwhelmed.[13]

Events of Instruction

Information processing models have had a substantial impact on librarians and other educators' approaches to the design of instructional situations. This influence can be seen in the work of Robert M. Gagné (1916–2002), an American educational psychologist who is often thought of as the father of instructional design. In major works such as *The Conditions of Learning* (1965) and *Principles of Instructional Design* (1974), Gagné described five varieties of learning—intellectual skills, cognitive strategies, verbal information, motor skills, and attitudes—and elaborated on the internal (i.e., within the learner) and external (i.e., within the instructional environment) conditions that are needed to achieve each of these types of learning.[14]

Gagné also elaborated on nine phases of information processing that are important for learning, which can be grouped into three broader phases, as shown in table 3.1.

TABLE 3.1

Gagné's nine phases of learning

Broader Phases	Phases of Learning
Preparing for Learning	1. Attending to the stimuli for learning 2. Establishing an expectation for what is to be learned 3. Activating what one already knows by retrieving relevant information in long-term memory
Acquisition and Performance	4. Selectively perceiving information 5. Encoding information in long-term memory 6. Retrieving that information to perform tasks 7. Processing feedback about what was learned
Transfer of Learning	8. Constructing cues for later recall 9. Generalizing the learning to new situations

Table compiled using the phases discussed in Robert M. Gagné, *The Conditions of Learning*, 3rd ed. (New York: Holt, Rinehart, and Winston, 1977), 284–86, and Margaret E. Gredler, *Learning and Instruction: Theory into Practice*, 6th ed. (Upper Saddle River, NJ: Pearson, 2009), 154–56.

Gagné believed that educators should design their instruction around these phases of learning. He described nine events of instruction that educators can use to guide them in the design of lessons that enhance learning. These are:

1. Gaining attention
2. Informing the learner of the objective
3. Stimulating the recall of prerequisite learning
4. Presenting the stimulus material
5. Providing learner guidance
6. Eliciting the performance
7. Providing feedback about performance correctness
8. Assessing the performance
9. Enhancing retention and transfer[15]

Attention plays a key role during both preparation for learning and acquisition and performance. During the preparation phase, attention can be understood in terms of an alertness to receive information. Often this occurs when learners physically orient themselves to the learning stimulus, as when they turn their heads to better look and listen. Librarians and other educators can use a variety of methods to alert learners to content to be learned, often by introducing a change into the environment, such as by using a different tone of voice, appealing to learners' interests, introducing a novel idea, or doing a different activity.[16]

During the acquisition and performance phase, attention can be understood in terms of *selective perception*, which describes the ways that a learner focuses on certain aspects of stimuli in order to facilitate processing in working memory. Because learners are limited as to the amount of information they can process at a time, they can use selective perception to filter out irrelevant content such as noise or enticing smells and focus on information to be learned. Librarians and other educators can aid in the process of selective perception by accentuating certain content. They can emphasize important information, ask questions, use graphic organizers, or tell learners to underline certain words and phrases in text. Librarians and other educators can also teach learners how to use features of media designed to accentuate key pieces of information. Specifically, text may contain headings and bold print, and demonstration videos may use arrows or highlighting to show learners what is most important.[17]

IMPLICATIONS FOR LIBRARIES

Libraries have become a refuge for learners who want to preserve their limited attentional resources. Librarians have an important role to play by providing spaces in which noises and other sensory stimuli are reduced, thus allowing people to read, study, and learn with minimal distractions. While learners have many needs for collaborative spaces in which they can speak and interact, librarians can balance these spaces with a variety of quiet spaces. In addition, librarians can promote healthy and productive uses of technologies that enhance learning without creating too many distractions.

Here are a variety of strategies that librarians can use to help learners focus their attention:

- Provide a variety of quiet spaces, from open floor spaces to private rooms. Make sure that quiet spaces are located sufficiently far away from noisy entryways. Provide signage that clearly delineates quiet spaces.

- Create rules for quiet spaces that prohibit talking or noise from cell phones, and enforce noise restrictions. Keep in mind that gentle background noise can sometimes help learners to focus if it resembles a quiet hum.
- Be aware of sights and sounds within library spaces that may help or hinder learners from focusing their attention. For example, do group study rooms contain video monitors that constantly show images? Are walls filled with clutter? If some library spaces allow for eating, consider establishing spaces that prohibit food consumption, as food smells can be highly distracting.
- Ensure that spaces are adequately lit to help learners focus. Natural lighting can provide enough light to allow learners to focus while reducing eye strain and improving feelings of well-being.
- Provide family-friendly spaces with books and toys where parents can bring their children to play and read while they focus on their own learning and study.
- Provide meditation rooms or other spaces for prayer or quiet contemplation.
- Hang pictures on walls or create in-person or online exhibits to attract attention to content that can enhance learning.
- Create library web content, instructional screenshots, or videos that provide visual cues (such as arrows or highlighting) and that make adequate use of contrast and white space to help focus learners' attention on important content.

TEACHING LIBRARIAN'S CORNER

During instruction, librarians can help to focus learners' attention by using *cues*, which provide a stimulus that directs focus. Librarians commonly use verbal cues, such as telling learners what they will be learning about or what types of content they need to attend to. But other types of cues can be used as well. For instance, librarians might use an image to capture learners' attention, or they might indicate certain types of information to watch for in a video. Images can be especially powerful because they are often more likely to be remembered than verbal information (see chapter 4, "Multimedia"). A librarian's movement and gestures can serve as visual cues as well.

While learners attend to information consciously in classroom situations, they may also attend unconsciously to other information from their environment, which can have an impact on their ability to learn. Thus, when teaching, librarians should try to minimize environmental distractions as much as possible.

Librarians can use some of the following strategies to capture and maintain learners' attention during instruction:

- At the start of a session, share instruction goals and agendas with learners so that they know what to focus on. During a session, indicate to learners the information that is most important for them to attend to (e.g., using phrases such as "Here you can see that . . .").
- Teach content at an appropriate level. Learners have trouble focusing when the content is above their heads, and they become easily distracted when the content is below their level.
- Introduce new or surprising information, use interesting or novel images, or incorporate new technologies or activities. Learners are often intrigued by novelty.
- "Read" the room during instruction. Look at learners' faces to monitor their attention and adjust instruction accordingly.
- Minimize distractions from the classroom environment (e.g., close the door if there is noise coming from the hallway). Make rules limiting cell phone usage during instruction, if necessary, or show learners how to use cell phones or other technologies in a productive manner.
- Divide large assignments into smaller chunks so that learners do not have to focus their attention on too much information at once (e.g., annotated bibliography assignments can help learners to focus on one source at a time before having to synthesize multiple sources in a research paper).
- Ask questions to help learners focus on important information from readings, videos, and other materials (e.g., "What is the problem that this author is trying to address?").
- Provide outlines, worksheets, and graphic organizers to help learners focus their attention. Incorporate different types of graphic organizers into instruction such as tables, concept maps, flow charts, tree diagrams, and bar charts. These types of tools can be used, for example, to help learners follow a series of instructions or identify the progression of ideas found in sources.

- Teach learners how they can use text features to decide what to focus on (e.g., headings and bolded words can help learners identify content to pay attention to in readings). Instruct learners to use underlining or highlighting to help them identify important parts of readings.

Using Theatrical Techniques to Direct Attention during Library Instruction

The theater provides many examples of techniques that teaching librarians can use in the classroom to attract learners' attention or direct their focus. Like actors, librarians can use their voices to direct attention to certain words and phrases by varying pitch, volume, and tone. They can direct attention using their bodies by moving around the room and incorporating gestures into their teaching, while keeping in mind that too much movement can be distracting. They can manipulate the lighting and sound in the classroom by playing music or lowering or raising the lights at appropriate times. Finally, they can attract attention by using comedy techniques, such as wearing a funny "costume" (e.g., colorful socks) or telling a joke, if appropriate. However, it is wise to approach the use of humor with thoughtfulness, as poorly chosen jokes can create awkward situations. Sometimes the use of self-deprecating humor may feel safer than telling jokes.

FURTHER READING

Carr, Nicholas G. *The Shallows: What the Internet Is Doing to Our Brains*. New York: W. W. Norton, 2010.

Gagné, Robert M., Walter W. Wager, Katharine Golas, and John M. Keller. *Principles of Instructional Design*. 5th ed. Belmont, CA: Cengage Learning, 2004.

Sousa, David A. *How the Brain Learns*. 6th ed. Thousand Oaks, CA: Corwin, 2022.

QUESTIONS TO CONSIDER

1. In what ways can technologies distract learners from focusing their attention? In what ways can technologies be used to help learners focus?

2. Choose a space within a library or other public place. How might the design of that space help or hinder learners in focusing their attention?

3. What are some strategies that librarians can use to manage distractions while teaching?

NOTES

1. Roger H. Bruning et al., *Cognitive Psychology and Instruction*, 4th ed. (Upper Saddle River, NJ: Pearson, 2004), 16.

2. David A. Sousa, *How the Brain Learns*, 5th ed. (Thousand Oaks, CA: Corwin, 2016), 41–42.

3. Sousa, *How the Brain Learns*, 43–48.

4. Bruning et al., *Cognitive Psychology and Instruction*, 28–29.

5. Sousa, *How the Brain Learns*, 109; Bruning et al., *Cognitive Psychology and Instruction*, 26–27.

6. George A. Miller, "The Magic Number Seven Plus or Minus Two: Some Limits on Our Capacity for Processing Information," *Psychological Review* 63 (1956): 91–97.

7. Sousa, *How the Brain Learns*, 47.

8. Sousa, *How the Brain Learns*, 48–49, 83–85.

9. Peter Klaver, "Attention," in *Encyclopedia of Neuroscience*, ed. Marc D. Binder, Nobutaka Hirokawa, and Uwe Windhorst (Berlin: Springer, 2009).

10. Nicholas G. Carr, *The Shallows: What the Internet Is Doing to Our Brains* (New York: W. W. Norton, 2010).

11. Carr, *The Shallows*.

12. American Psychological Association, "Multitasking: Switching Costs," March 20, 2006, www.apa.org/topics/research/multitasking.

13. Edward Hallowell, "Overloaded Circuits: Why Smart People Underperform," *Harvard Business Review*, January 1, 2005, https://hbr.org/2005/01/overloaded-circuits-why-smart-people-underperform.

14. Robert M. Gagné, *The Conditions of Learning*, 3rd ed. (New York: Holt, Rinehart, and Winston, 1977), 25–50; Robert M. Gagné, Leslie J. Briggs, and Walter W. Wager, *Principles of Instructional Design*, 4th ed. (Fort Worth, TX: Harcourt Brace Jovanovich, 1992), 53–98.

15. Gagné, Briggs, and Wager, *Principles of Instructional Design*, 185–204.

16. Gagné, *The Conditions of Learning*, 63, 68–69, 292–93.

17. Gagné, *The Conditions of Learning*, 52–53, 63–64, 68–69, 292–93.

MULTIMEDIA

THEORETICAL OVERVIEW

Because of modern technologies, it is easier than ever to incorporate images into instructional situations, and images can play a powerful role in learning. In fact, *multimedia learning* revolves around the notion that learners can better understand information when it is presented through both words and images than through words alone.[1] Multimedia learning factors heavily into the kinds of technologies and services that libraries offer, the incorporation of technologies into library spaces, the design of the online delivery of information content, and the use of multimedia during library instruction and outreach events.

Current understandings of multimedia learning have been greatly influenced by information processing theories, which describe the ways that information is ingested, filtered, and coded through aspects of the sensory, working, and long-term memory system (see chapter 3, "Attention"). American psychologist Richard E. Mayer and his colleagues have described much of the theory and application behind multimedia learning.[2] Their work on multimedia learning has been heavily influenced by the concepts of cognitive load and dual coding, which explain some of the factors at play when humans process visual and textual information from their environments.

Cognitive Load

Cognitive load was initially described by Australian educational psychologist John Sweller and his colleagues in the 1980s.[3] *Cognitive load theory* explains the capacity limits of working memory, which concerns the conscious processing of new information in the short-term memory system. Simply put, if some types of cognitive load become too high, then learning becomes difficult. Thus, cognitive load theory has implications for the ways that instruction is designed in order to facilitate more effective processing of information in working memory.

Cognitive load theory explains the importance of schemas for learning. Schemas are mental organization patterns held in long-term memory that facilitate learning (see chapter 1, "Constructing Knowledge"). Because schemas make information processing more efficient by aiding with the limited processing capacity of working memory, they can aid learning. Schemas help to reduce cognitive load by processing a collection of information through a single mental pattern. In other words, schemas provide a means through which multiple information elements are coded as one single element. As an example, a theater artist might have a mental schema for dramatic works that includes several elements, such as exposition, rising action, climax, and resolution. This schema may make it easier for the artist to understand and remember plays than for someone who does not have this mental framework.

In fact, experts in particular fields have developed domain-relevant schemas that allow them to process information more efficiently. Experts grow their proficiency in a particular domain by combining lower-level schemas to create more complex, higher-level schemas that continue to function as a single element, thereby increasing their mental processing capacity in that domain.[4]

Furthermore, many schemas become automated through repetition so that they require fewer resources in working memory, freeing up capacity to allow more information to be processed. While tasks such as reading or doing simple math equations can be mentally taxing on young children, they require minimal processing power for adults who have learned to automate these processes.

Cognitive load theory suggests that librarians and other educators should help learners construct schemas to improve their information processing abilities. The process of constructing schemas plays into different types of cognitive load: intrinsic cognitive load, extraneous cognitive load, and germane cognitive load (see table 4.1).

Librarians and other educators cannot do much to alter the intrinsic cognitive load of certain tasks, although they can present a series of related tasks progressing from easier to more difficult, provide tools such as notes and graphic organizers that aid learning, and provide scaffolding support to help learners master easier tasks before moving on to more difficult ones. However, they have greater ability to affect extraneous or germane cognitive load through their instructional design

TABLE 4.1 **Types of cognitive load**

TYPE OF COGNITIVE LOAD	SOURCE	DESCRIPTION	EXAMPLE
Intrinsic cognitive load	Caused by the intrinsic nature of the content or task	Intrinsic cognitive load is often a result of the complexity of the task or material, which results from the interconnection of multiple components. Skills that are difficult to learn have a high intrinsic cognitive load.	The skill of synthesizing multiple sources comes with a high intrinsic cognitive load because it requires a learner to summarize the argument and main ideas of individual sources, compare them to other sources, and identify similarities and differences.
Extraneous cognitive load	Caused by mental processing requirements that are unrelated to learning	Extraneous cognitive load often results from poor instructional design or information presentation that takes mental capacity away from learning. Extraneous cognitive load can be caused by busy multimedia tools or videos that overwhelm the learner with images and sounds unrelated to learning, or by classroom instruction that requires learners to engage in unhelpful activities such as interpreting confusing instructions.	Using a poorly designed database may increase extraneous cognitive load by forcing a learner to grapple with how to use the system, taking mental resources away from focusing on good information search strategies.
Germane cognitive load	Related to processes that enhance learning	Germane cognitive load often results from the process of constructing schemas for learning and automating those schemas, which help learners process information more effectively.	A librarian might teach the use of filters in research databases by drawing comparisons to the use of filters in online shopping websites in order to activate learners' existing search schemas and increase germane cognitive load.

Table compiled using concepts found in Paul A. Kirschner, Femke Kirschner, and Fred Paas, "Cognitive Load Theory," in *Psychology of Classroom Learning: An Encyclopedia*, ed. Eric M. Anderman and Lynley H. Anderman, vol. 1, 2 vols. (Detroit: Gale Cengage Learning, 2009), 206–8.

choices. Librarians and other educators should attempt to decrease extraneous cognitive load (i.e., reduce elements that take away from learning) and increase germane cognitive load (i.e., improve factors that assist with learning).

The presentation of content through multimedia may serve to either increase or decrease extraneous and germane cognitive load. Moreover, multimedia learning concerns the notion that cognitive capacity can be increased by presenting information in more than one modality, a process which is described by dual coding theory.

Dual Coding

Dual coding theory, which was developed by Canadian psychologist Allan Paivio and his colleagues in the 1970s, addresses the unique role that language plays in the way that humans process, understand, and remember information.[5] According to *dual coding theory*, external information is represented in mental forms in memory through two distinct systems, one for verbal and one for nonverbal information (see figure 4.1):

- The *verbal coding system* involves the coding of any type of textual information. This can include words received through various senses, such as spoken or written language or through motor movements such as the feel of Braille or the articulation of words.
- The *nonverbal* or *imagery coding system* involves the coding of pictures, sounds, tastes, and other nonverbal information received through the senses. Because the processing and generation of images plays a major role in the nonverbal system, it is often referred to as the imagery or imaginal system.[6]

Both systems contribute to the development of understanding.

The two systems differ in some respects. Information in the verbal system is processed individually—that is, each word is processed one at a time. Verbal information is also processed sequentially—that is, the letters in a word and the words in a sentence have to be processed in a particular order for their meaning to be understood.[7] For example, the words in the sentence "The books are located on the second floor" are processed individually and in order. If the words in the sentence are rearranged, their meaning is more difficult to comprehend.

On the other hand, information in the imagery system is processed spatially or synchronously. In other words, a single image may contain many individual details that can be processed simultaneously.[8] For instance, a photo of the second floor

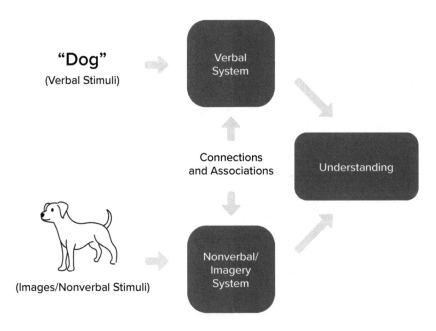

FIGURE 4.1

The verbal and nonverbal coding systems

of a library may contain images of shelves, books, tables, chairs, and other items that can be received and understood at the same time. This characteristic difference between the verbal and imagery processing systems provides support for the adage "a picture is worth a thousand words" because images can, in fact, be mentally coded for greater amounts of information.

These two systems can operate independently and simultaneously. Furthermore, information from one system can connect to or generate information in the other and vice versa. People make connections between these two systems by mentally associating verbal and nonverbal codes, which can aid in learning and memory. For example, when they hear the word "dog," they might call forth an image of a running German shepherd. Likewise, when they see a playing Chihuahua or hear a bark, they might think the word "dog."

Another important difference between the two systems is that abstract ideas can be represented through the verbal system, whereas concrete objects or events can be represented through either the imagery or verbal systems.[9] Words that represent concrete items (e.g., "scales") will often have greater power to trigger associated images than words that represent abstract concepts (e.g., "justice"). This means that concrete words that instantly call forth images in the mind of a reader or listener (e.g., "drooling dog") activate both imagery and verbal representations simultaneously, making them easier to remember than abstract language (e.g., "behavioral psychology"). In addition, many images are often already dual coded. For example, when a learner sees an image of a book, they may also mentally think the word "book." Librarians and other educators can take advantage of this associative tendency by using images in their instruction or by encouraging learners to generate their own mental images when learning concepts.

Dual coding theory suggests that because verbal and nonverbal information are coded through separate mental processing systems, information that is presented using both words and images can be better understood and remembered than information that is presented through words alone.

Multimedia Learning Design

Multimedia learning theory describes the ways that instructional content can be effectively presented using both text and graphics. Words can include either printed or spoken text, and graphics can include pictures, graphs, maps, videos, and other types of static or moving images.

Multimedia learning facilitates the processes of both remembering and understanding information—that is, using information to construct meaning. When learning through multimedia materials, learners select words and images for processing in working memory and organize them independently into verbal or visual constructions. Not only can more information be processed when it is presented through both the verbal and imagery channels, but the material can be processed differently in each channel, so that some aspects of the material to be learned can be better presented using words whereas other aspects can be better presented using images, allowing the two modes to complement each other. After creating internal verbal and visual knowledge structures, learners can then integrate them into a single mental model for greater understanding.[10] This suggests that instructional multimedia messages should have clear structures or provide guidance for how learners can create their own mental schemas for processing information.

While dual coding theory asserts that learners may benefit when verbal and visual forms of information are presented together, cognitive load theory suggests that there are limits to the amount of information that can be processed in each channel at a time. Mayer and Ruth C. Clark have outlined several principles to guide the design of multimedia use in instruction, with attention to maximizing dual coding potential while managing cognitive load. A few of these principles are listed in table 4.2 (on page 42).

IMPLICATIONS FOR LIBRARIES

Many current pedagogies, including those offered in online environments, are dependent on the use of multimedia technologies. Specifically, collaborative learning activities (described in chapter 2, "Collaboration") often involve group presentations that are created and shared using programs such as Microsoft PowerPoint. In addition, flipped classroom pedagogy involves having learners review course content—delivered using multimedia formats such as videos and interactive lessons—prior to coming to class. Class time is then used for active and collaborative learning activities. School, academic, and public libraries can provide spaces, technologies, and services that support these new multimedia pedagogies, and librarians can provide and create multimedia learning content as well.

Here are a variety of strategies that librarians can use to support multimedia learning:

- Provide access to a variety of multimedia collections that support learning, and promote these collections with educators.
- Provide access to technologies that allow learners not only to read text but also to listen to audio, watch videos, and create their own media content. Provide high-tech spaces that allow for various types of media creation.
- Provide media equipment that learners can check out to complete projects.
- Make technologies available in collaborative learning spaces that allow learners to view and create presentations together.
- Offer in-person and online training in how to use media technologies. Offer training for educators in ways to incorporate images and media into instruction.
- Subscribe to resources that provide online courses in media and technology skills.
- Create instructional web content that follows multimedia design principles.
- Incorporate images and multimedia elements into event planning, marketing, and advocacy materials. Keep the graphics in these materials simple and uncluttered.

TABLE 4.2

Principles for designing instructional multimedia materials

PRINCIPLE	EXPLANATION	RATIONALE	GUIDANCE FOR CREATING MULTIMEDIA MATERIALS
Contiguity principle	Place words as close as possible to their corresponding graphics.	When words and images are placed far apart on a single page, are presented at different times, or are presented using separate media (such as a book and video), then the learner's attention is divided and more mental resources must be used to coordinate between text and image.	Pictures should be placed as close as possible to the words that they illustrate, and text should be integrated into illustrations or animations. Spoken narration should play at the same time that a graphic is viewed so that both are as "close" together as possible, which encourages learners to make connections between the two, resulting in better understanding of the material.
Coherence principle	Avoid adding unnecessary text, sounds, or images to material.	Adding superfluous text or images—such as animated GIFs, background music, cutesy stories, or unnecessarily complicated graphs—may interfere with learning because they often require learners to use extra mental processing resources to absorb this information.	Graphics should be used that help to convey meaning and encourage learners to create mental schemas, such as by depicting relationships among the elements to be learned or providing an organization for the elements. Multimedia material should be clear and uncluttered.
Signaling principle	When multimedia presentations contain a lot of information, add verbal or visual cues to signal where to focus attention.	Complex graphics such as dynamic animations can be mentally taxing because they present a great deal of visual information.	Use visual cues, such as arrows or highlighting, to help learners know where to focus in an image. Use auditory cues, such as added vocal emphasis or signal phrases (e.g., "Notice how"), to help learners know what to listen for.

Principle			
Modality principle	If possible, present text that accompanies images using audio rather than print.	When images and printed text are presented together, a learner has to direct their attention either to looking at the images or reading the words; they cannot attend to them both at the same time.	When presenting image and text together, present the text in spoken form, so that learners can process it through the auditory channel rather than the visual channel. In this manner, text does not compete for mental processing power with images, which may reduce cognitive load.
Pretraining and segmenting principles	Include pretraining content, which is explanatory material presented at the beginning of a lesson, and break lessons into smaller parts.	When complex material is presented in multimedia formats, learners' intrinsic cognitive load can become overwhelmed.	Present key terms and definitions at the beginning of the lesson to help learners process them, while saving cognitive resources for more complex material that is presented later on. Break content into segments or steps to ensure that learners mentally process each part before moving on to the next.
Generative activity principle	Integrate learning activities that are designed to enhance deep engagement with the material.	Completing generative learning activities helps to combat the sometimes overwhelming nature of multimedia content and allows time and space for deep mental processing.	Include activities that enhance understanding of the material, such as summarizing, mapping, drawing, or self-testing.

Table compiled using concepts found in Ruth Colvin Clark and Richard E. Mayer, *E-Learning and the Science of Instruction: Proven Guidelines for Consumers and Designers of Multimedia Learning*, 4th ed. (Hoboken: Wiley, 2016), and Richard E. Mayer, *Multimedia Learning*, 3rd ed. (Cambridge: Cambridge University Press, 2020).

TEACHING LIBRARIAN'S CORNER

The incorporation of multimedia into instructional materials offers numerous opportunities for librarians to be creative with lesson plan construction and delivery. Librarians can incorporate greater use of imagery into presentation slides, use graphic organizers to help learners understand information, and encourage learners to use mental imagery to help them grasp complex processes.

At the same time, more is not necessarily better. While technologies may make instructional materials more visually appealing, they should only be used to support the goals of the lesson. Too much incorporation of multimedia (e.g., excessive animations or music) can overwhelm learners' abilities to mentally process what they are receiving. For example, dynamic animations are not necessarily more effective than static animations (e.g., drawings).[11] Moreover, the more complex the instructional material (e.g., videos and interactive tutorials), the more difficult they are to produce, so librarians should think carefully before investing the time and resources to create complex multimedia materials.

Librarians can use some of the following strategies to incorporate multimedia learning theory into their teaching:

- Create library instructional materials such as handouts, web pages, online learning modules, and videos that incorporate both images and text.
- Keep slides and other presentation material uncluttered. Avoid placing too much text on slides, as fewer words may be easier to process. Keep charts and graphs as simple as possible. Avoid adding decorative or unnecessary content.
- Use concrete examples and images that elicit strong verbal associations to help learners understand and remember concepts (e.g., an image of tracks in the snow could represent the concept of following the citation trail; an image of a chessboard could represent the concept of forming a strategy for planning a research project).
- Teach strategies for smart image and video searching so that learners can incorporate visual media into their projects.
- Teach strategies for interpreting and analyzing images for use as research sources to help learners develop deeper understandings of their subject matter (e.g., noticing details in an image, considering

textual information that accompanies an image, considering the meanings conveyed by an image, considering how design choices contribute to an image's meaning).[12]

- When using video during lessons, incorporate questions so that learners receive guidance about what to pay attention to and how to process the information they are viewing.
- Encourage learners to create visuals or graphics to represent concepts or ideas from information sources (e.g., creating a poster that conveys the major parts of a research article or completing a table that compares ideas from different information sources).
- Encourage learners to create visualizations to help them understand concepts (e.g., ask learners to draw the research process or create a concept map to visualize the parts of a topic).
- When creating instructional materials with complex images or videos (e.g., demonstrations of database search interfaces), use visual cues such as arrows or highlighting to help learners know where to focus their attention.
- When creating videos or interactive tutorials, introduce key concepts and definitions early in the material (e.g., the meaning of "full text" in database searching or the format of empirical research articles). Insert knowledge check questions or other activities at key points so as to prompt learners to stop and process what they have learned so far.

FURTHER READING

Clark, Ruth Colvin, and Richard E. Mayer. *E-Learning and the Science of Instruction: Proven Guidelines for Consumers and Designers of Multimedia Learning.* 4th ed. Hoboken, NJ: Wiley, 2016.

Mayer, Richard E. *Multimedia Learning.* 3rd ed. Cambridge: Cambridge University Press, 2020.

Paivio, Allan. *Mental Representations: A Dual Coding Approach.* New York: Oxford University Press, 1986.

QUESTIONS TO CONSIDER

1. Choose a particular library or research assignment for a learner of your choice. Describe the three types of cognitive load listed in this chapter and give an example of each as it might relate to learning the material for that assignment.

2. Choose a specific type of library. What kinds of training sessions could the library offer to its patrons to help them learn to better use and understand multimedia materials?

3. Choose a concept related to information literacy or some other area of interest. How might this concept be represented visually in instructional materials?

NOTES

1. Richard E. Mayer, *Multimedia Learning* (Cambridge: Cambridge University Press, 2001), 1.

2. Ruth Colvin Clark and Richard E. Mayer, *E-Learning and the Science of Instruction: Proven Guidelines for Consumers and Designers of Multimedia Learning*, 4th ed. (Hoboken, NJ: Wiley, 2016); Richard E. Mayer, *Multimedia Learning*, 3rd ed. (Cambridge: Cambridge University Press, 2020).

3. John Sweller, Jeroen J. G. van Merriënboer, and Fred Paas, "Cognitive Architecture and Instructional Design: 20 Years Later," *Educational Psychology Review* 31, no. 2 (June 2019): 261–92, https://doi.org/10.1007/s10648-019-09465-5; John Sweller, Jeroen J. G. van Merriënboer, and Fred G. W. C. Paas, "Cognitive Architecture and Instructional Design," *Educational Psychology Review* 10, no. 3 (September 1998): 251–96, https://doi.org/10.1023/A:1022193728205; J. J. G. van Merriënboer and J. Sweller, "Cognitive Load Theory and Complex Learning: Recent Developments and Future Directions," *Educational Psychology Review* 17, no. 2 (2005): 147–77, https://doi.org/10.1007/s10648-005-3951-0.

4. Paul A. Kirschner, Femke Kirschner, and Fred Paas, "Cognitive Load Theory," in *Psychology of Classroom Learning: An Encyclopedia*, ed. Eric M. Anderman and Lynley H. Anderman, vol. 1, 2 vols. (Detroit: Gale Cengage Learning, 2009), 205–9.

5. Allan Paivio, *Mental Representations: A Dual Coding Approach* (New York: Oxford University Press, 1986); Allan Paivio, *Mind and Its Evolution: A Dual Coding Theoretical Approach* (Mahwah, NJ: Lawrence Erlbaum Associates, 2007); James M. Clark and Allan Paivio, "Dual Coding Theory and Education," *Educational Psychology Review* 3, no. 3 (1991): 149–210, https://doi.org/10.1007/BF01320076; Mark Sadoski and Allan Paivio, *Imagery and Text: A Dual Coding Theory of Reading and Writing*, 2nd ed. (New York: Routledge, 2013), https://doi org/10.4324/9780203801932.

6. Roger H. Bruning et al., *Cognitive Psychology and Instruction*, 4th ed. (Upper Saddle River, NJ: Pearson, 2004), 53–54; Sadoski and Paivio, *Imagery and Text*, 42–66; Paivio, *Mental Representations*, 53–83.

7. Clark and Paivio, "Dual Coding Theory and Education."

8. Clark and Paivio, "Dual Coding Theory and Education."

9. Clark and Paivio, "Dual Coding Theory and Education."

10. Mayer, *Multimedia Learning*, 2020, 29–62.

11. Clark and Mayer, *E-Learning and the Science of Instruction*, 97.

12. Nicole E. Brown et al., *Visual Literacy for Libraries: A Practical, Standards-Based Guide* (Chicago: American Library Association, 2016).

OBSERVATION

THEORETICAL OVERVIEW

Imagine trying to hit a serve in tennis, whip up a meringue, solve a math problem, or operate scientific lab equipment without first watching how someone else did it. Trying to do these tasks without first being able to observe them would be difficult. *Observational learning* describes the process whereby people learn by watching others and seeing the consequences of those behaviors.[1] Libraries are places where people often learn through observation, and librarians frequently model positive behaviors for learners to imitate.

The importance of observational learning was described by Canadian American psychologist Albert Bandura as part of his social cognitive theory of behavior. In this theory, Bandura elaborated upon a number of constructs that have become central to current understandings of how learning occurs, including self-efficacy, modeling, and self-regulation. The first two are discussed below, while self-regulation is further discussed in chapter 6.

Social Cognitive Theory

Bandura elaborated on his social cognitive theory in a series of books that began appearing in the 1960s, including *Social Learning Theory* (1977), *Social Foundations of Thought and Action: A Social Cognitive Theory* (1986), and *Self-Efficacy: The Exercise of Control* (1997). *Social cognitive theory* stresses that learning occurs within a social environment and that people learn by observing the behaviors of others and the consequences of those behaviors. While previous theorists had described how people either influenced their environments or the environments influenced people, they generally explained this process as occurring in one direction. Bandura noted that people's relationships with their environments was more complex. According to him, learning occurs through a *triadic reciprocality* between personal and cognitive factors (e.g., thoughts, emotions, personality traits), environmental factors (e.g., culture, physical environment, social environment), and behaviors (e.g., actions, speech); that is, each of these three factors interacts with and influences the others (see figure 5.1).[2]

This model of triadic reciprocality ascribes a powerful role to a person's own agency in learning, as the three factors are constantly influencing each other. For example, in a library instruction session, a librarian might teach a student how to conduct database research on a topic of the student's choosing. In this case, an environmental factor—that is, the lesson provided by the librarian about how to select a research topic and search a database—influences a personal and cognitive factor—a student's topic selection and understanding of database search strategies. As the student begins to search (behavior) on a topic of interest to them (person/cognition), they might have trouble finding suitable research (environment), which may necessitate that the librarian teaches additional search skills or new databases that present the student with new strategies to try (environment). As the student

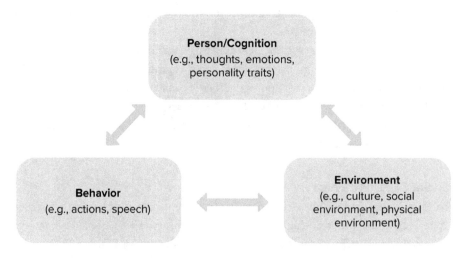

FIGURE 5.1

Bandura's concept of triadic reciprocality

continues searching (behavior), they might become interested in a different topic (person/cognition) and decide to pursue this instead. Thus, the continual interaction that occurs among the person/cognition, behavior, and the environment affect and shape the learning process.

Environment and cognition do not operate with equal influence on behavior at all times. Sometimes the environment provides a stronger influence, while at other times person/cognition is stronger. Similarly, people can recognize the powerful influence that the environment has on their behavior and choose to modify it, knowing that this will force them to change their thinking and behavior (e.g., deciding not to keep chocolate in one's home to prevent oneself from thinking about sweets and overindulging, or going to a library to ensure that one studies a difficult subject).

Before Bandura developed his social cognitive theory, it was thought that learning largely occurred through performance enactments, whereby learners execute behaviors related to specific knowledge and skills. With *enactive learning*, learners perform actions and experience the consequences of their actions, which may be positive or negative, enjoyable or unenjoyable. The experience of these consequences prompts learners to repeat, alter, or avoid the behavior.

However, Bandura described how learners also learn through vicarious learning; that is, observation. He described the importance of observation for learning:

> Learning would be exceedingly laborious, not to mention hazardous, if people had to rely solely on the effects of their own actions to inform them what to do. Fortunately, most human behavior is learned observationally through modeling: from observing others one forms an idea of how new behaviors are performed, and on later occasions this coded information serves as a guide for action.[3]

Through observation, people learn about many things that they have never directly experienced or enacted. Observation can provide a means through which people learn behaviors, knowledge, concepts, rules, and values.[4]

Unlike enactive learning, observational learning allows people to learn without directly experiencing the consequences. In other words, learners can watch others, observe the consequences that they experience, and learn what behaviors to repeat or avoid. As an example, when a learner observes a librarian successfully retrieve data, create an art project, or operate equipment for making, they may see positive consequences ensue, which may make them more likely to repeat the behaviors they witnessed. At the same time, if a learner witnesses a student in a makerspace who makes an error that causes their project to break, they may avoid mimicking that behavior. Not only will learners choose to repeat or avoid behaviors based on the consequences that ensue to the observed actors, but they may also make decisions based on whether those behaviors align with their interests and values.

Observational learning is not only important and efficient, but it is even necessary for survival. Bandura explained:

> Because mistakes can produce costly, or even fatal consequences, the prospects for survival would be slim indeed if one could learn only from the consequences of trial and error. For this reason, one does not teach children to swim, adolescents to drive automobiles, and novice medical students to perform surgery by having them discover the requisite behavior from the consequences of their successes and failures. The more costly and hazardous the mistakes, the heavier must be the reliance on observational learning from competent exemplars.[5]

The importance of observation suggests that the environment, and the way that learners interact with it, plays an important role in learning. Both observation and action are important and necessary methods of learning, and both enactive and vicarious learning factor strongly into Bandura's conception of self-efficacy.

Self-Efficacy

As Bandura's model of triadic reciprocality demonstrates, personal agency is critical for learning. Therefore, a learner's perceived efficacy has an important influence on their ability to learn successfully. *Self-efficacy* describes the belief in one's ability to execute certain tasks in order to achieve certain outcomes.[6] Self-efficacy is essentially about confidence; in other words, does a learner feel confident in their ability to successfully execute certain tasks? Bandura described how "beliefs of personal efficacy constitute the key factor of human agency. If people believe they have no power to produce results, they will not attempt to make things happen."[7]

Thus, self-efficacy does not necessarily concern a learner's knowledge and skills but their belief that they are capable of using their knowledge and skills to accomplish particular tasks. Self-efficacy is therefore not tied to a learner's objective assessment of their abilities, but is instead more closely associated with their feelings, thought patterns, and self-regulatory strategies, as well as environmental cues and past experiences.

A learner's efficacy expectations can be distinguished from their *outcome expectations*, which are judgments that certain actions will result in certain consequences.[8] For instance, a learner designing a presentation may know that making excellent choices about visuals may have a strong impact on their audience (outcome expectations), but they may not feel that their own visual design skills will allow them to achieve this (efficacy expectations). Similarly, self-efficacy, which describes one's confidence in one's abilities, differs from self-esteem, which describes a person's assessment of their own worth.[9] A learner may have low self-esteem but high self-efficacy related to a particular skill, and the opposite may be true as well.

Self-efficacy also relates closely to a learner's motivation to take on difficult tasks, as well as their determination to work hard and persist in the face of challenges. Learners with stronger efficacy beliefs will be more inclined to use self-regulating strategies, manage their own stress reactions, maintain a positive attitude toward learning, and learn from past mistakes.[10] Learners with these positive self-perceptions are confident in their ability to achieve successful outcomes. However, if learners do not believe they can do something, then they will not even try.

Bandura identified four main sources of self-efficacy.[11] Not only are the sources important in and of themselves, but the ways that learners interpret information from these four sources are critical for how they affect perceived efficacy.

1. *Mastery experiences* are performance accomplishments. Learners who have successfully completed tasks in the past will have stronger beliefs about their ability to complete similar tasks in the future. When learners experience repeated successes, they feel more confident in their abilities, but repeated failures will have the opposite effect. However, repeated successes at easy tasks are not enough. Instead, learners must experience success with challenging tasks in order to bolster their confidence that they can succeed at similar challenging tasks in the future. For example, a student who is assigned to write a research paper will feel more confident in their ability to complete it if they have previously written a research paper and received a good grade on the assignment. Mastery experiences are the strongest source of self-efficacy because "they provide the most authentic evidence of whether one can muster what it takes to succeed."[12]

2. *Vicarious experiences* occur when learners observe others completing similar tasks. Learners may gain confidence by observing models who successfully work through similar challenges, but they may lose confidence when they see others fail. Competent models will tend to exert greater influence than those who are incompetent and will help to establish what success looks like. For example, a graduate student writing a dissertation may gain confidence by working with a mentor who models the inquiry process and serves as an example of achievement. Quite often people learn from observing their peers perform in similar situations, which provide points of social comparison and measures of success.

3. *Verbal persuasions* are messages that learners receive about their ability to accomplish certain tasks. Verbal persuasions can be positive and encouraging—potentially strengthening self-efficacy—or negative and discouraging—potentially weakening it. Just as learners may be more influenced by observing competent models, they may also be more strongly persuaded when verbal messages come from those perceived as competent or skilled. For example, a learner struggling with a design project may feel more confident in their abilities if a much admired teacher offers words of encouragement about their current progress as well as suggestions about how they can build on this progress during the next steps. In fact, verbal persuasions are most effective when they do not consist of empty praise but are genuine and honest, designed to help learners accurately assess and improve their abilities. At the same time, negative messages, whether intentional or not, can have a negative impact on self-efficacy.

4. *Physiological and emotional states* are learners' own internal moods and emotions. Physiological and emotional states include responses to stress and anxiety, as well as the positive and negative emotional reactions and moods that often accompany the learning process and influence motivation. While positive affective states may strengthen feelings of efficacy, negative affective states may weaken it (see chapter 8, "Affect"). Not only do the physiological and emotional states themselves affect perceived efficacy, but perceived efficacy can in turn affect a learner's physiological and emotional states. For example, learners with a strong sense of efficacy related to their research skills may be more successful at managing stress and harnessing their emotions when they are assigned a large research project, while learners with lower research efficacy may be more prone to feeling overwhelmed with anxiety when they receive the same assignment. Because these physiological and emotional states are highly subjective, the ways that learners interpret and respond to these states may also affect self-efficacy. Some learners may view certain types of pressure or physiological arousal as motivating, whereas others may view it as debilitating.

Modeling

People learn vicariously by observing teachers, librarians, friends, media figures, or other models. *Modeling* describes the process whereby people think, believe, or act on the basis of what they observe in others.[13] In a classroom situation, observational learning commonly occurs when learners observe the behaviors of teachers and peers. Teachers frequently model behaviors that they want learners to imitate, often with accompanying explanations.

Modeling can occur through several methods. Librarians and other educators can use live demonstrations, words, graphic organizers, and images, and the choice to use each of these will depend upon the behaviors being modeled, the characteristics of the learners, and the situations in which learning occurs. Librarians and other educators can use a number of different modeling strategies as well:

- *Mastery modeling:* Models provide a competent and successful demonstration of a task.
- *Coping modeling:* Models show how to work through challenges when completing a task. They may make errors, explain why they are having trouble, demonstrate how to work through difficulties, and exemplify persistence.
- *Cognitive modeling:* Models use "think aloud" techniques to explain a process while demonstrating it. They may show multiple examples of how to approach a task while providing rationales for their choices.
- *Abstract modeling:* Models demonstrate rules or principles that observers must then transfer to other situations.[14]

An important factor in the effects that a model's behavior has on learning involves the consequences of the observed behavior. Some modeled behaviors will result in positive effects that encourage the observer to try to imitate them. Other modeled behaviors will result in negative consequences that serve to inhibit or weaken an observer's likelihood of repeating the behaviors. Learners may be more strongly influenced by observing actions that lead to success, but they can learn from seeing failures as well.

Bandura also described four processes through which observational learning occurs:

1. *Attention:* Learners attend to the behaviors of the model.
2. *Retention:* Learners code the observed behavior into memory through words or images. Often learners use a process of mental rehearsal to review the observed skill.
3. *Production:* Learners translate what they remember about the observed behavior into action. Often learners attempt an action, process feedback about it, and then try again.

4. *Motivation:* Learners feel motivated to reproduce the modeled behavior. Learners will be more motivated to imitate behaviors that they perceive as having positive outcomes or that are consistent with their values and goals.[15]

The qualities of a particular model can also influence a learner's receptiveness. Learners are more likely to be attentive to and learn from models who are skilled, successful, or prestigious.[16] Learners are also inclined to learn from models whom they perceive as being similar to themselves, since their actions are ones that they are more likely to do too.[17] In a school situation, this means that learners may be attentive to behaviors modeled by children or adolescents of a similar age or background. These behaviors can consist of academically relevant tasks such as how to complete a particular homework assignment, as well as other ways of acting, such as how to dress. In libraries, seeing a peer do research or use technology successfully can be motivating, leading other learners to believe that they can overcome challenges to succeed. Exposing learners to different types of models can also be useful, depending upon the learning situation.

Finally, Bandura was one of the first theorists to note the influential role that mass media play in learning. Observational learning is not solely confined to seeing models in "real life." Instead, people learn from *symbolic models* that appear through various media, such as television or movies. Because of the wide reach of the media and because of the often attractive qualities of those images, the media play a powerful role in observational learning.[18] While Bandura was focused on the influential effects of observing symbolic models through mass media such as television advertising, in today's environment people "observe" the actions of those on social media and may learn from the consequences of behaviors that are portrayed on these platforms, which are often misrepresented.

IMPLICATIONS FOR LIBRARIES

The power of observation helps to explain why people come to a social setting such as a library to read or study. Bandura noted that "people applaud when others clap, they laugh when others laugh, they exit from social events when they see others leaving, and on countless other occasions their behavior is prompted and channeled by modeling influences."[19] In other words, seeing others engaged in an activity can make one more inclined to do the same. By coming to libraries where they can surround themselves with positive examples of others engaged in learning and study, learners often attempt to ensure that they will learn and study too.

Librarians can use some of the following strategies to help people learn through observation:

- Design library spaces to allow learners to observe others engaged in positive learning activities, such as using whiteboards to create outlines or complete math problems.
- Provide media collections that contain video or other sources that include models performing tasks (e.g., videos that demonstrate how to hold different types of counseling sessions for counseling students).
- Incorporate peer learning strategies into library reference, instruction, and outreach services so that learners can observe peer models.
- Use the library website or the school's learning management system to provide recorded or written demonstrations of library tasks that learners need to accomplish.
- When planning events, invite speakers who can model skills and values that will benefit learners.
- Use modeling during outreach events to show users specific skills, such as read-aloud strategies, presentation skills, or primary source usage.
- Create pop-up learning spaces in the library where library staff can give quick demonstrations that model library skills for learners.

TEACHING LIBRARIAN'S CORNER

Librarians can use a number of instructional techniques to maximize the learning potential of observation and provide learners with opportunities to increase their self-efficacy. Modeling is commonly used to teach library-related skills, and librarians may frequently model skills during instruction sessions without even realizing it.

Librarians can use the following strategies to enhance their use of observational learning and promote self-efficacy in learners during instruction:

- Model behaviors that build on what learners already know so that they are more likely to be able to reproduce the newly learned skills.
- Vary the types of modeling strategies used, such as coping modeling or mastery modeling, and incorporate the use of mnemonic devices, graphic organizers, or step-by-step instructions into modeling.
- Use strategies to draw learners' attention to the skill to be modeled, such as using interesting images or emphasizing the importance of a lesson for academic success.

- Model strategies that increase learners' sense of self-efficacy with finding and using information for research projects, such as following the citation trail and creating an organizational plan.[20]
- Invite learners to model their research and other skills for their peers.
- Alternate the provision of observational learning with enactive experiences. Follow modeled skills with activities to give learners a chance to practice.
- Provide clear guidance or structure when giving large assignments or tasks so that learners feel confident about how to execute them.
- Help learners to anticipate when they may encounter difficulties with a task and teach them strategies for managing their own physiological and emotional states when they encounter those difficulties.
- Give feedback to learners after they have reproduced the modeled activity and allow them to repeat, correct, and refine it. Use positive but sincere verbal messages to help increase learners' self-efficacy regarding challenging tasks.

Modeling during Library Instruction

Librarians can improve their use of modeling during instruction by becoming aware of the different types of modeling and by varying their use depending on the instructional situation and the needs of learners. As an example, during instruction, a librarian might model the process of forming a research topic for a paper and beginning to search for information about it. She might start by role-playing the process of selecting a topic: "My brother has peanut allergies, and I'm very interested in learning more about why that is." She then thinks aloud as she describes how to approach the topic: "I think it would be helpful to know how common food allergies are and who is likely to have them. Which types of foods usually cause allergies? And are there any treatments available?"

As she continues, she incorporates the various types of modeling. She talks learners through her thought process as she brainstorms different research angles and keywords for searching (cognitive modeling). In addition to verbalizing her thoughts, she writes a table of keywords and synonyms on a whiteboard and begins to search a database. As she searches, she comments upon her search results to indicate whether or not the results are relevant. She might demonstrate a perfect search that brings up many useful results (mastery modeling). But if her search resulted in failure, then she might demonstrate how to alter her strategy when initial searching is unsuccessful (coping modeling). As she searches, she might demonstrate principles such as Boolean searching before asking learners to apply them to other search situations (abstract modeling).

FURTHER READING

Bandura, Albert. *Self-Efficacy: The Exercise of Control*. New York: W. H. Freeman, 1997.

Bandura, Albert. *Social Foundations of Thought and Action: A Social Cognitive Theory*. Upper Saddle River, NJ: Prentice Hall, 1986.

QUESTIONS TO CONSIDER

1. What types of skills would be suitable for librarians to teach using modeling? How can modeling be used during library outreach events? Give some examples.

2. In what types of library instruction situations would it be appropriate to use mastery, coping, cognitive, or abstract modeling? Give some examples.

3. How might librarians promote the value of peer models?

NOTES

1. Albert Bandura, *Social Learning Theory* (Englewood Cliffs, NJ: Prentice Hall, 1977), 22, 25; Albert Bandura, *Social Foundations of Thought and Action: A Social Cognitive Theory* (Upper Saddle River, NJ: Prentice Hall, 1986), 47.

2. Bandura, *Social Foundations of Thought and Action*, 23–28.

3. Bandura, *Social Learning Theory*, 22.

4. Bandura, *Social Foundations of Thought and Action*, 47, 100.

5. Bandura, *Social Foundations of Thought and Action*, 20.

6. Albert Bandura, *Self-Efficacy: The Exercise of Control* (New York: W. H. Freeman, 1997), 3.

7. Bandura, *Self-Efficacy*, 3.

8. Bandura, *Self-Efficacy*, 19–24.

9. Bandura, *Self-Efficacy*, 11–13.

10. Bandura, *Social Foundations of Thought and Action*, 393–99; Bandura, *Self-Efficacy*, 791–94.

11. Bandura, *Self-Efficacy*, 79–115; Bandura, *Social Foundations of Thought and Action*, 399–409.

12. Bandura, *Self-Efficacy*, 80.

13. Dale Schunk, *Learning Theories: An Educational Perspective*, 8th ed. (New York: Pearson, 2019), 130; Bandura, *Social Learning Theory*, 22.

14. Bandura, *Social Learning Theory*, 39–50; Bandura, *Social Foundations of Thought and Action*, 100–105; Schunk, *Learning Theories*, 105–6; Christopher A. Wolters and Maria B. Benzon, "Social Cognitive Theory," in *Psychology of Classroom Learning: An Encyclopedia*, ed. Eric M. Anderman and Lynley H. Anderman, vol. 1, 2 vols. (Detroit: Gale Cengage Learning, 2009), 214–19; Marie C. White, "Cognitive Modeling and Self-Regulation of Learning in Instructional Settings," *Teachers College Record* 119, no. 13 (2017): 1–26; Barry J. Zimmerman, "From Cognitive Modeling to Self-Regulation: A Social Cognitive Career Path," *Educational Psychologist* 48, no. 3 (2013): 135–47, https://doi.org/10.1080/00461520.2013.794676.

15. Bandura, *Social Foundations of Thought and Action*, 51–80.

16. Bandura, *Social Foundations of Thought and Action*, 51–54.

17. Schunk, *Learning Theories*, 141.

18. Bandura, *Social Foundations of Thought and Action*, 70–72.

19. Bandura, *Social Learning Theory*, 87.

20. Ann Medaille et al., "Honors Students and Thesis Research: A Study of Information Literacy Practices and Self-Efficacy at the End of Students' Undergraduate Careers," *College & Research Libraries* 82, no. 1 (2021): 92–112, https://doi.org/10.5860/crl.82.1.92.

6

SELF-REGULATION

THEORETICAL OVERVIEW

A college student receives an assignment to write a research paper that is due in six weeks. She makes a plan for the project, which includes finding sources early, reading at least one source a week, and writing a little bit every week. She considers how confident she feels in her research and writing skills, and makes appointments with a librarian and writing tutor for assistance with areas of difficulty. As she reads through her sources, she recognizes that some sources are more challenging than others, and so she adapts her reading strategies as needed, identifying which parts require more careful reading and which parts can be skimmed. After she completes the assignment, she reflects on areas that caused her the most difficulty and considers how she might change her approach to a similar assignment in the future.

All of these activities involve self-regulated learning. *Self-regulated learning* is the process of mobilizing one's own thoughts, feelings, and actions in order to achieve learning goals.[1] Self-regulation is essential for learning in school settings and the workplace, and it is important for lifelong learning and personal development as well. Librarians can help to foster self-regulation by incorporating the language and practices of self-regulated learning into a variety of library activities.

Beginning in the 1980s, scholars began to describe models of self-regulation and to elucidate the ways that self-regulatory processes involve the integration of metacognitive awareness, the use of cognitive strategies, and motivational and affective engagement in learning. Because motivation and affect are addressed in detail in chapters 7 and 8, they are not described in this chapter. Instead, a discussion of metacognition provides a good place to begin a focus on self-regulation.

Metacognition

Cognition refers to higher-level thinking associated with the acquisition and use of knowledge, and it involves processes such as understanding, reasoning, and analyzing.[2] The prefix *meta* is commonly used to describe something that goes beyond or reflects upon itself. Thus, *metacognition* is, in a sense, thinking about thinking. Contemporary research into metacognition was begun in the 1970s by developmental psychologists John Flavell and Ann L. Brown, among others, although precursors can be found in Jean Piaget's description of cognitive conflict (discussed in chapter 1, "Constructing Knowledge") and Lev Vygotsky's description of the zone of proximal development[3] (discussed in chapter 13, "Guidance"). Flavell defined metacognition as "one's knowledge concerning one's own cognitive processes and products or anything related to them,"[4] and Brown defined it as "the deliberate conscious control of one's own cognitive actions."[5]

While cognition involves the acquisition of knowledge, metacognition involves understanding and managing how that knowledge is acquired. To do this effectively, a learner must give deliberate attention to the act of learning and the internal mental processes that it involves. Metacognitive processes help a learner to make assessments about the difficulty of a learning task, decide what information to pay attention to, choose strategies that will facilitate learning, and adjust those strategies if learning becomes difficult. Thus, metacognitive skills are closely associated with learning and achievement, and these skills can be learned and improved with practice.

Brown described how learners develop metacognitive knowledge about themselves by knowing *when* they do or do not know something (i.e., knowing when they succeeded or failed to understand information); knowing *what* they know (i.e., being aware of the knowledge they already have, how that knowledge can be applied, and the limits of that knowledge); and knowing what they *need to know* (i.e., identifying what knowledge is needed to accomplish certain tasks and when cognitive strategies are needed).[6]

Metacognition consists of two major components: understanding cognition and regulating cognition. The first relates to understanding the thinking process in general, understanding one's own distinct qualities as a learner, and understanding the characteristics associated with specific learning tasks. It includes three different types of knowledge:

1. *Declarative knowledge* consists of knowing things (e.g., facts or ideas). In relation to metacognition, declarative knowledge refers to knowing about certain aspects of the learning task or process and about oneself as a learner (e.g., knowing that background knowledge helps facilitate understanding when reading challenging material, or knowing that one has a strong memory for details or has trouble learning abstract concepts).

2. *Procedural knowledge* consists of knowing how to do things. In relation to metacognition, procedural knowledge refers to knowing strategies for learning (e.g., knowing how to take notes, highlight text, or identify main ideas when reading new material).

3. *Conditional knowledge* consists of knowing when and why to apply procedural knowledge. In relation to metacognition, conditional knowledge refers to knowing when and why to apply different strategies for learning (e.g., recognizing how different texts require the use of different reading strategies to understand and remember them).[7]

The second major component, regulating cognition, consists of three activities that occur before, during, and after thinking or learning: planning, monitoring, and evaluating:[8]

- *Planning* involves selecting cognitive strategies and allocating mental resources to those activities. Planning strategies can be enhanced by asking questions about the goal, the nature of the task, the strategies to use, and the time, information, and resources needed. For a learner who is searching for and reading information sources in order to complete an assignment, planning includes setting goals for an information search session, considering what they already know about a topic, and making predictions about what they will find.

- *Monitoring* involves checking one's progress while learning and altering strategies as necessary. Monitoring strategies can be enhanced by asking questions about whether the task and process make sense, whether the goal is being achieved, and whether changes need to be made. For the learner described above, monitoring strategies involve self-testing one's understanding of a topic and adjusting one's strategies when reading information sources turns out to be more or less difficult than initially thought.

- *Evaluating* involves appraising the outcome of learning. Evaluating strategies can be enhanced by asking questions about whether the goal was achieved, what worked or did not, and what processes should be changed. For the learner described above, evaluating strategies include revising one's approach to an assignment in light of the information one found, and comparing what one learned from the sources with one's own predictions.

Thus, as these descriptions of planning, monitoring, and evaluating demonstrate, an important component of learning to regulate one's thinking is understanding and using cognitive strategies.

Cognitive Strategies

A *cognitive strategy* is a mental process used to facilitate the achievement of a cognitive or learning goal.[9] Learners deliberately use cognitive strategies to aid thinking, and different learning situations call for the use of different cognitive strategies. While cognitive strategies are a type of procedural knowledge, their successful use requires that the learner possess conditional knowledge about how best to apply them and under what circumstances they should be applied.

Cognitive strategies relate to different aspects of learning. Some are methods that help the learner better remember or organize information. Some help with planning for learning, managing time or resources, or managing emotions during learning. Still others relate to specific types of learning tasks, such as reading sources or doing math problems. Some types of cognitive strategies and the tasks they relate to are listed in table 6.1.

While learners may discover some cognitive strategies on their own, quite often they need to learn about them, as well as how best to apply them and how to evaluate their effectiveness. For instance, learners often do not know how best to study for and review material for tests and other assessments, and thus they can benefit from learning strategies for effective studying. While cognitive strategies may initially be used with great attention and deliberation, they may also become automatic with practice, which results in less of a drain on the cognitive resources needed for learning new knowledge and skills. The use of cognitive strategies and continual metacognitive monitoring are crucial components of self-regulated learning.

The Self-Regulatory Process

The process of self-regulated learning has several characteristics. First, it is an active process during which a learner takes responsibility for their own learning

TABLE 6.1

Select cognitive strategies and tasks

Cognitive strategies for evaluating information sources	Cognitive strategies for understanding material found in information sources
• Identifying the purpose and audience of a source • Identifying an author's credentials • Identifying an author's argument and opposing arguments • Determining whether evidence has been used to support an argument • Identifying language that indicates bias • Identifying corroborating sources	• Taking notes from sources • Underlining and highlighting information in sources • Summarizing • Paraphrasing • Asking and answering questions while reading • Using graphic organizers to organize information from sources • Adjusting the pace of reading to the demands of different kinds of texts • Using text structures (i.e., headings, topics sentences) to facilitate understanding • Identifying main ideas
Cognitive strategies for writing papers	**Cognitive strategies for projects involving making skills**
• Dividing the paper into smaller segments • Creating a timeline for completion • Finding a quiet place to write • Identifying when more information is needed • Writing an outline before beginning a draft • Making connections between new information and what one already knows • Grouping similar ideas together • Rereading what has been written aloud to aid revision	• Defining an idea or problem • Brainstorming products or solutions • Drawing or mapping ideas • Breaking a larger project into smaller parts or steps • Recording measurements in advance • Developing a timeline for completion • Recording project notes for future use • Requesting help from experts

and deliberately uses techniques to enhance it. Second, it is a goal-driven process during which a learner sets goals and then works toward achieving those goals. Third, because self-regulation is fundamentally a learner- and goal-driven process, it is unique to the learner, being strongly affected by a learner's own personal characteristics, beliefs, and arsenal of cognitive strategies.

While scholars have developed several models of self-regulated learning, one of the most commonly referenced models comes from Barry J. Zimmerman,[10] who described how self-regulation occurs through an iterative process of three main phases, correlated to what happens before, during, and after learning occurs.

The *forethought* phase includes understanding the learning task, setting goals for completion, breaking large tasks into smaller chunks, and selecting cognitive strategies to meet these goals. This phase is influenced by learners' goal orientations (see chapter 7, "Motivation"), self-efficacy (see chapter 5, "Observation"), interest in the task, and the value they place on the task. For example, if a learner is planning to make a craft project, some tasks in the forethought phase might include brainstorming ideas, drawing a project plan or design, laying out all of the materials needed ahead of time, and creating a timeline for completion.

During the *performance* phase, learners use various strategies to help them learn, including focusing their attention, managing their time, structuring their environment, engaging in positive self-talk, and getting help. They exhibit metacognitive awareness by monitoring their own performance and the shifting demands of the task to determine whether they are meeting their goals, and they adjust their use of cognitive strategies as needed. For instance, a learner who is making a craft project may pivot to the use of different supplies if they cannot get an item needed, manage their frustration if a piece breaks, or request assistance if they encounter a problem.

In the *self-reflection* phase, learners evaluate their performance in relation to a standard and determine whether their strategies were effective in meeting or failing to meet their goals. In reflecting upon the success of their experience, learners assign causal attributions for their performance (see chapter 7, "Motivation") and process affective responses to their experiences. These self-reflections are then funneled back into and subsequently influence the forethought phase during the learner's next enactment of the self-regulatory process during another learning task. For example, a learner who is making a craft project will measure their progress against their initial design, assess what they might have done differently, and feel increased motivation to do another project if they feel proud of their work.[11]

In learning to self-regulate, the social environment plays an important role. This was first described by Vygotsky, who elaborated on the ways that children first learn speech as a way of communicating with other members of society but then internalize it and use it to regulate their own thought processes (see chapter 2, "Collaboration"). He also described how children are aided by a more knowledgeable person who guides their learning and helps them achieve tasks they initially could not do on their own (see chapter 13, "Guidance"). After receiving assistance, children are eventually able to perform tasks independently using their own self-regulatory strategies to guide them.[12]

Bandura also identified a prominent role for social and environmental influences in the development of self-regulation in his social cognitive theory (see chapter 5, "Observation"). Social cognitive researchers have described four stages through which people learn to self-regulate, as shown in table 6.2 (on page 68). This self-regulatory process begins outside of the learner through the observation of models and then moves inward as the learner internalizes the process and uses it independently. As learners transition from observing and emulating models to using and adapting the skills on their own, their self-efficacy increases, which in turn influences their willingness to set their own goals and use their own self-regulatory strategies in the future.[13]

Finally, learners may not use self-regulatory strategies all the time for all learning situations, but they may vary their degree of self-regulation depending on the situation and learning goal.

IMPLICATIONS FOR LIBRARIES

Self-regulation is essential for lifelong learning. Lifelong learning adds richness to people's lives as they experience the joy of pursuing their own interests. While learners are often guided by their own passions and motivations when pursuing their personal learning and development goals, self-regulatory strategies can enhance their learning experiences by giving them the tools to pursue complex cognitive tasks on their own. Libraries often play an important role in supporting lifelong learning goals.

Furthermore, many libraries support workplace development initiatives, and self-regulated learning is important for these contexts as well. Learners who hope to improve their workplace skills often need to use self-regulatory strategies to help them balance learning with other life commitments and persist in the face of challenges, including the technical challenges that come with staying up-to-date in many professions. Self-regulatory strategies can support these workplace development goals as well.

TABLE 6.2

Four stages of learning to self-regulate

STAGE	DESCRIPTION	EXAMPLE
Observation	Learners observe models using self-regulatory strategies in the performance of tasks.	Learners observe a librarian modeling the process of working through challenges encountered during a search for demographic data.
Emulation	Learners attempt to replicate self-regulatory strategies used by models and may receive feedback from models on their use.	Learners create their own concept maps of topics, based on what they observed a librarian doing, and the librarian provides feedback.
Self-control	Learners perform self-regulatory strategies with a greater sense of autonomy, using their mental ideas of how the model behaves as a guide.	After learning about time management strategies in a library workshop, learners create their own timelines for completing a major project.
Self-regulation	Learners have fully internalized self-regulatory strategies and are able to use and adapt them based on the learning task and the situational demands.	Given a choice of how to present the results of research using different media, learners decide upon a format and set goals for its completion, getting help from a librarian or media specialist if they determine that they are running into trouble and altering strategies as needed.

Table compiled from concepts found in Ellen L. Usher and Dale H. Schunk, "Social Cognitive Theoretical Perspective of Self-Regulation," in *Handbook of Self-Regulation of Learning and Performance*, ed. Dale H. Schunk and Jeffrey A. Greene, 2nd ed. (New York: Routledge, 2018), 19–35, and Dale H. Schunk and Barry J. Zimmerman, "Social Origins of Self-Regulatory Competence," *Educational Psychologist* 32, no. 4 (1997): 195–208, https://doi.org/10.1207/s15326985ep3204_1.

Librarians can use some of the following strategies to support self-regulated learning:

- When giving library workshops, incorporate opportunities for learners to set goals for what they hope to learn at the beginning and to reflect upon what they learned at the end.

- Provide training in or information about technologies that help learners to self-regulate (e.g., time management apps, productivity apps).
- Subscribe to resources that cater to lifelong learners (e.g., language learning programs) or contain self-regulatory or time management features (e.g., research project planners, methods maps). Provide instruction in how to use these tools.
- Create and share templates that learners can use for guidance during research, media, and maker tasks (e.g., source evaluation worksheets, project timelines, concept maps).
- Incorporate events into library programming that emphasize stress management and emotional well-being.
- Emphasize the importance of help-seeking for lifelong learning. Encourage learners to get help when they run into trouble and make a variety of help services readily available (e.g., in-person, online, technology help, research help).
- Encourage peers to model self-regulatory strategies skills when assisting other learners during consultations, and teach them how to do so.
- Promote studying and learning in the library as a self-regulatory strategy that learners can use when they find that other settings they encounter are filled with distractions that inhibit learning.

TEACHING LIBRARIAN'S CORNER

Librarians can find many opportunities to incorporate self-regulatory strategies into the teaching of information, digital, making, and other skills. This can include a variety of self-regulatory strategies, including planning, monitoring, reflecting, using positive imagery and self-talk, managing one's time, getting help, using external resources, and adjusting to the environment. Librarians should teach and model the strategies themselves and give learners opportunities to practice applying these strategies in different settings and for different tasks. Finally, librarians can give learners feedback about their use of self-regulatory strategies, which in turn can help to increase motivation and self-efficacy.

Librarians can use some of the following strategies to incorporate self-regulated learning theory into instruction:

- Give learners the opportunity to set their own goals for an assignment, project, or course and encourage them to create project plans and timelines.

- Instruct learners in how to break down larger goals into smaller goals to be achieved along the way.
- Model different cognitive strategies, including positive motivational and affective states, and "think aloud" so that learners can better understand the thought processes behind them. Devise opportunities for learners to practice different cognitive strategies, and give them feedback.
- Teach techniques for using cognitive strategies to understand source material (e.g., techniques for paraphrasing source material or identifying main and supporting ideas).
- Teach learners how to use self-regulatory tools such as planners, schedules, search logs, source notes, and graphic organizers.
- Ask questions that prompt learners to self-monitor their learning, and teach them some strategies for evaluating their own performance.
- After completion of a learning task, give learners prompts for reflective writing that ask them to respond to different features of the learning task and the final outcome (e.g., Did they encounter challenges with identifying a research question? Were they able to find relevant images to use as sources? Were they able to identify bias in sources?).
- Prompt learners to reflect upon the appropriateness and effectiveness of different cognitive strategies in different disciplinary contexts (e.g., strategies for primary source analysis for history projects, strategies for evaluating images for use in design projects).

FURTHER READING

Cleary, Timothy J. *The Self-Regulated Learning Guide: Teaching Students to Think in the Language of Strategies*. New York: Routledge, 2018. https://doi.org/10.4324/9781315693378.

Hartman, Hope J. *Metacognition in Learning and Instruction: Theory, Research and Practice*. Dordrecht, Neth.: Kluwer Academic, 2001.

Schunk, Dale H., and Jeffrey A. Greene, eds. *Handbook of Self-Regulation of Learning and Performance*. 2nd ed. New York: Routledge, 2018.

QUESTIONS TO CONSIDER

1. Identify an assignment a learner might receive that is related to library resources or research processes. What are the planning, monitoring, and evaluating activities that might be associated with that assignment? What metacognitive questions could learners ask themselves in order to help regulate their own learning?

2. What are some ways that a librarian could integrate instruction about cognitive strategies into a lesson? Provide some examples.

3. In what ways can technologies support or undermine learners' attempts to self-regulate? Provide some examples.

NOTES

1. Barry J. Zimmerman, "Becoming a Self-Regulated Learner: An Overview," *Theory into Practice* 41, no. 2 (2002): 64–70, https://doi.org/10.1207/s15430421tip41 02_2; Ellen L. Usher and Dale H. Schunk, "Social Cognitive Theoretical Perspective of Self-Regulation," in *Handbook of Self-Regulation of Learning and Performance*, ed. Dale H. Schunk and Jeffrey A. Greene, 2nd ed. (New York: Routledge, 2018), 19–35.

2. Alan Pritchard, *Ways of Learning: Learning Theories and Learning Styles in the Classroom*, 3rd ed. (London: Routledge, 2014), 29–30.

3. Linda Baker, "Metacognition," in *Psychology of Classroom Learning: An Encyclopedia*, ed. Eric M. Anderman and Lynley H. Anderman, vol. 2, 2 vols. (Detroit: Gale Cengage Learning, 2009), 604–8.

4. John H. Flavell, "Metacognitive Aspects of Problem Solving," in *The Nature of Intelligence*, ed. Lauren B. Resnick (Hillsdale, NJ: Lawrence Erlbaum Associates, 1976), 232.

5. Ann L. Brown, "Metacognitive Development and Reading," in *Theoretical Issues in Reading Comprehension: Perspectives from Cognitive Psychology, Linguistics, Artificial Intelligence, and Education*, ed. Rand J. Spiro, Bertram C. Bruce, and William F. Brewer (Hillsdale, NJ: Lawrence Erlbaum Associates, 1980), 453.

6. Brown, "Metacognitive Development and Reading," 453–81.

7. Gregory Schraw, "Promoting General Metacognitive Awareness," in *Metacognition in Learning and Instruction: Theory, Research and Practice*, ed. Hope J. Hartman (Dordrecht, Neth.: Kluwer Academic, 2001), 3–16; Scott G. Paris, Marjorie Y. Lipson, and Karen K. Wixson, "Becoming a Strategic Reader," *Contemporary Educational Psychology* 8, no. 3 (1983): 293–316, https://doi.org/10.1016/0361-476 X(83)90018-8.

8. Janis E. Jacobs and Scott G. Paris, "Children's Metacognition about Reading: Issues in Definition, Measurement, and Instruction," *Educational Psychologist* 22, no. 3–4 (1987): 255–78, https://doi.org/10.1080/00461520.1987.9653052; Schraw, "Promoting General Metacognitive Awareness."

9. Clark A. Chinn and Lisa M. Chinn, "Cognitive Strategies," in *Psychology of Classroom Learning: An Encyclopedia*, ed. Eric M. Anderman and Lynley H. Anderman, vol. 1, 2 vols. (Detroit: Gale Cengage Learning, 2009), 209–14; Michael Pressley and Karen R. Harris, "Cognitive Strategies Instruction: From Basic Research to Classroom Instruction," in *Handbook of Educational Psychology*, ed. Patricia A. Alexander and Philip H. Winne, 2nd ed. (Mahwah, NJ: Routledge, 2006), 265–86.

10. Zimmerman, "Becoming a Self-Regulated Learner"; Barry J. Zimmerman, "From Cognitive Modeling to Self-Regulation: A Social Cognitive Career Path," *Educational Psychologist* 48, no. 3 (2013): 135–47, https://doi.org/10.1080/00461520.2013.794676.

11. Usher and Schunk, "Social Cognitive Theoretical Perspective of Self-Regulation"; Zimmerman, "Becoming a Self-Regulated Learner."

12. Dale Schunk, "Self-Regulated Learning," in *Psychology of Classroom Learning: An Encyclopedia*, ed. Eric M. Anderman and Lynley H. Anderman, vol. 2, 2 vols. (Detroit: Gale Cengage Learning, 2009), 806–9.

13. Usher and Schunk, "Social Cognitive Theoretical Perspective of Self-Regulation"; Dale H. Schunk and Barry J. Zimmerman, "Social Origins of Self-Regulatory Competence," *Educational Psychologist* 32, no. 4 (1997): 195–208, https://doi.org/10.1207/s15326985ep3204_1.

MOTIVATION

THEORETICAL OVERVIEW

Motivated learners are eager to learn, and they are attentive to the content to be learned. They have a positive attitude toward learning and attempt to learn on their own. They try hard, embrace learning challenges, and persist when things get difficult. Libraries often provide the resources, tools, and activities that stimulate learners' interests and motivate them to fully engage in the learning process.

Motivation describes a learner's willingness to engage in goal-oriented activity.[1] The state of motivated activity involves both cognitive and affective engagement in tasks. Motivation relates closely to learners' emotions, interests, values, beliefs, and personal assessments, as well as to the features of the environments in which learning occurs. While there are many theories of motivation, three that are especially relevant for libraries are discussed below: achievement goal theory, self-determination theory, and attribution theory.

Achievement and Performance Goals

While it has its antecedents in early twentieth-century research, achievement goal theory was developed in the late 1970s and early 1980s by Carole Ames, Carol S. Dweck, and others.[2] An achievement goal describes the purpose with which a learner engages in tasks. Thus, achievement goal theory describes how learners who are engaged in similar academic tasks may have different underlying motivations that influence their emotions, their learning strategies, and the success of their learning endeavors.

Achievement goal theory, also known as goal orientation theory, conceptualizes two primary motivators of learner behavior in academic contexts: mastery and performance. Learners with a *mastery goal orientation* are primarily interested in learning—that is, they are interested in improving their skills. Learners with a *performance goal orientation* are primarily interested in demonstrating competence in comparison with others—that is, they are interested in proving their skills. Mastery goals are sometimes referred to as *learning goals*, while performance goals are sometimes referred to as *ego goals*.

Learners who have a mastery goal orientation engage in tasks because they want to develop their abilities and acquire new knowledge; in other words, they want to achieve mastery in learning content or skills. They put forth effort to improve and generally believe that hard work can lead to success. They tend to view challenges as an opportunity for growth and do not shy away from pursuing difficult tasks. They value learning for the inherent joys it brings and tend to maintain a positive attitude toward learning, even in the face of setbacks.

Learners with a mastery goal orientation often judge their progress on the basis of how they have improved over time. They tend to use metacognitive and self-regulatory strategies to gauge their own learning and work toward improvement. Mistakes or failures are often viewed as an indication that they need to change their learning strategies or put forth more effort. They often experience a sense of control over their learning, which results in feelings of pride and self-efficacy when they reach their goals. They feel confident that their efforts will pay off, which contributes to increased motivation, persistence, and long-term engagement.

Learners who have a performance goal orientation engage in tasks because they want to demonstrate their abilities, perform well in comparison to others, and receive recognition for their accomplishments. Success is measured in terms of doing as well as possible with as little effort as possible. They may avoid engaging in challenging tasks if there is a risk of failure. They may be interested in either appearing competent or avoiding the appearance of incompetence. They might choose to engage in tasks that they believe make them look good and avoid those tasks that make them look "stupid."

Learners with a performance goal orientation often judge their progress on the basis of social comparisons. Some learners with performance goals may even employ adverse strategies, such as failing to get help when needed to avoid appearing less competent than their peers. They may believe that mistakes are viewed as indications of their inadequacy and threats to their self-esteem, and they may therefore blame their failures on causes such as procrastination. If they do not perform well in comparison with others, they may feel bad about themselves and feel less control in academic situations, which contributes to less persistence and decreased motivation.

Achievement goal orientations are closely related to different views of intelligence.[3] Dweck first described how some learners hold an *entity view of intelligence*, believing that ability is a fixed quality that is difficult—if not impossible—to change. Learners who hold an entity view of intelligence may be more likely to have performance goals because they want to demonstrate that their ability is acceptable. If they fail, they may also be more likely to feel that they are helpless to change the situation in the future. Learners who have an *incremental view of intelligence* believe that they can increase their ability with learning and effort. Learners who hold an incremental view of intelligence are more likely to have mastery goals and to see academic challenges as opportunities to grow and improve their skills.

While it is generally thought better to have a mastery goal orientation, there may be times when having performance goals can be motivating, such as when having to learn content that one finds boring or uninteresting. In addition, learners may have both mastery and performance goal orientations either simultaneously or when engaging in different tasks. Changing goal orientations may also help learners to vary their criteria for success depending on the situation and task.[4]

While learners' own personal characteristics may play a role in their goal orientations, the actions of educators and the overall learning environment may encourage learners to develop certain goal orientations. When librarians and other educators emphasize grades or comparisons with others, then learners may be more likely to develop a performance goal orientation. When librarians and other educators focus on the joys of learning and praise learners' efforts, then they may be more likely to develop a mastery goal orientation.

Intrinsic and Extrinsic Motivation

Another way to understand the role of motivation in learning relates to *intrinsic motivation*, which is characterized by engagement in tasks for the joy and pleasure that come from the activity itself. When learners are intrinsically motivated, they pursue challenges that are inherently interesting to them.

Intrinsic motivation is positively linked to learning and achievement. Intrinsic motivation is often contrasted with *extrinsic motivation*, which describes engagement in tasks in order to obtain a reward that is external to the task itself. In learning environments, extrinsic rewards may consist of grades, praise from a teacher, recognition for achievement, a prize for completion, or approval from peers.

Edward L. Deci and Richard M. Ryan explained the importance of intrinsic motivation in the 1980s in their *self-determination theory*, which describes three main human needs:

- *Competence:* the need to be capable and skilled
- *Autonomy:* the need to be in control of and feel a sense of agency regarding one's actions
- *Relatedness:* the need to feel connected to people and to feel that one belongs to a group or community[5]

When all three of these needs are met, learners may experience self-determination, which is the process of using their will to enact behaviors that satisfy their needs.[6] Self-determination leads to increased interest and engagement in learning. When learners do not experience the sense of choice and control that comes with self-determination, their intrinsic motivation to engage in tasks may decrease.

Some learners who are engaged in activities that are intrinsically motivating may even experience *flow*, which is the "state in which people are so involved in an activity that nothing else seems to matter."[7] Flow was first explained by psychologist Mihaly Csikszentmihalyi beginning in the 1970s. When experiencing flow, learners are concentrating so intensely on an activity that they may lose awareness of time. They become so engrossed that they experience little self-consciousness, worry, or fear of failure.

The state of flow often occurs when learners have acquired enough skill in a particular area that they do not have to struggle with basic functions. Once learners can competently draw, play the piano, play tennis, or do some other activity, they may find that they enter into this state of total absorption. Learners may achieve a flow state when the degree of challenge of an activity is well-matched to their abilities. When the degree of challenge is greater than a learner's skill level, then they may become stressed. When a learner's skill level is greater than the degree of challenge, then they may become bored or relaxed.[8] Flow represents this ideal meeting of ability and challenge (see figure 7.1).

While intrinsic motivation is usually thought to be better than extrinsic motivation, the latter can still serve useful purposes in regard to the self-regulation of learning behavior. In fact, learners may be simultaneously both intrinsically and extrinsically motivated. There are also different kinds of extrinsic motivation, which can be understood on a continuum from internalization to externalization. At one end of the continuum, *identified* motivation describes the way a learner executes tasks because they are valuable or important to their identity or to achieving

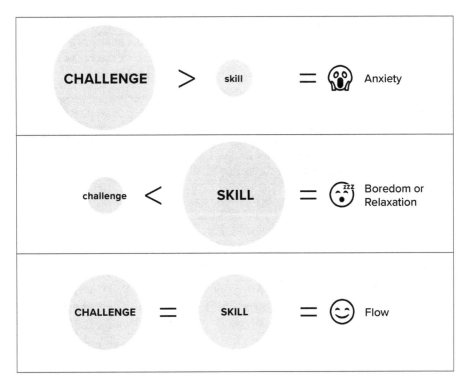

FIGURE 7.1

Relation of skill level to challenge level

their goals. With *introjected* motivation, a learner does a task because they feel that they should. With *external* motivation, a learner does a task to receive an external reward or avoid an external punishment.[9]

Librarians and other educators can help to increase learners' intrinsic motivation by sparking their curiosity with new or surprising information, by appealing to their imagination, by giving them greater control over their own learning, and by designing tasks with the appropriate level of challenge. Librarians and other educators can also use external rewards to motivate learners when they do not have much intrinsic interest in an activity or when they need to learn basic skills that can subsequently increase their engagement. However, sometimes these external rewards may serve to undermine learners' intrinsic motivation because they tie control of the activity to the external reward itself, which may decrease a learner's sense of self-determination.[10]

Recognizing Student Motivations

A university librarian is working with an undergraduate honors student who is doing original research on a local Indigenous language. The librarian recognizes how several types of motivations and goal orientations are present within the student:

> The student describes how she loves studying the intricacies of different languages (intrinsic motivation). She enjoys the challenge of learning how to analyze and mark up a language (mastery goal orientation). She plans to work with her professor to publish her work (external motivation) and hopes that her work can give back to the local community, which is important to her (identified motivation). But she is worried that she may be falling behind with her research timeline, and she feels that she should be working harder (introjected motivation). She's heard from several of her peers that they are further ahead with their research projects and she wants to keep up (performance goal orientation).

Causal Attributions

While achievement goal theory focuses on the reasons why learners engage in tasks in the first place, attribution theory centers on learners' beliefs about actions that have occurred in the past. Attribution theory has been most thoroughly explicated by Bernard Weiner, an American psychologist who wrote extensively about it beginning in the 1970s.[11]

Attribution theory describes how people seek to understand the causes of behaviors that have resulted in particular outcomes. People are always wondering why certain events occurred. In determining the causes of behaviors, people observe that certain behaviors resulted in success or failure, and they feel emotions (e.g., happiness, surprise, disappointment, dejection) in response to these outcomes. After experiencing emotions related to particular outcomes, people seek to know why success or failure occurred—that is, they look for a cause. In learning situations, success and failure are most commonly attributed to ability, effort, luck, task ease or difficulty, and assistance or hindrance from others, but mood, illness, fatigue, personality, personal appearance, and teachers may also be the ascribed causes.[12]

This assessment of causes is a subjective process that is based on various sources of information and is heavily influenced by perception and emotion. While learners' causal assessments may be either accurate or inaccurate, these assessments motivate their future behaviors.

Weiner identified three major dimensions of attributions:

1. *Locus:* whether the cause is internal or external to the individual
2. *Stability:* whether the cause is constant or varying over time and situations
3. *Controllability:* whether or not the cause can be controlled by the individual[13]

Locus has a powerful influence on self-perception, since an assessment of internal causes related to talent, skill, or intelligence can affect a learner's self-esteem and confidence, which in turn affects their motivation. Causes such as ability, effort, illness, and mood have an internal locus, but causes such as luck and task difficulty have an external locus.

Stability influences future outcome expectations. If the attributed causes are stable, then a learner is likely to believe that a similar outcome will occur again. Causes such as luck and illness are unstable, but causes such as ability and task difficulty are stable. If success with executing tasks is attributed to stable causes, then learners may be motivated to engage in those tasks in the future, believing that continued positive outcomes are likely. Similarly, failure attributed to stable causes can be demotivating because stable causes would suggest that continued future negative outcomes are likely.

Finally, controllability also influences a learner's decision to engage in certain tasks. Causes such as effort are controllable. When learners attribute positive outcomes to controllable behaviors such as working hard and using good learning strategies, then they may determine that their actions are more likely to result in continued academic achievement, a causal assessment that increases motivation. But when they attribute negative outcomes to uncontrollable causes, such as their intelligence, then they may feel demotivated from engaging in similar tasks in the future. Learners who believe that they have control over their successes are more likely to work hard, persist when things get difficult, and have high performance.

A learner's assessment of the causes of the outcomes and the accompanying dimensional factors will generate more emotions in the learner, such as pride in one's effort and ability, embarrassment about one's lack of ability, guilt at not trying harder, or relief that the task was not as difficult as one anticipated (further discussed in chapter 8, "Affect"). These emotions will then factor into a learner's perception of the likelihood of future success or failure, making them more or less motivated to engage in similar tasks in the future.

Making Causal Assessments

A high school student who completes an assignment to use library resources in writing a research paper might make different causal assessments depending on the outcome:

- If the student receives a positive grade on the assignment, he might determine that he is a skilled researcher and writer, that his hard work paid off, or that the help he received from his teacher and librarian factored into his success.
- If the student receives a poor grade on the assignment, he might determine that he is a poor writer, that the assignment was too difficult, that he did not receive adequate instruction, or that he did not try hard enough.
- If the student had written previous papers and received a higher grade on this paper, then he might attribute the cause to his own hard work. But if he learns that his grade was lower than that of other students, then he might decide that either he is not as capable or he did not try hard enough.

The student's interpretation of these causes will then influence his feelings about writing research papers and his subsequent motivation to write them in the future.

IMPLICATIONS FOR LIBRARIES

Libraries should be places where learners feel motivated to learn about topics and engage in activities that are of interest to them. Librarians can host events, lead projects, and initiate collaborations that encourage learners to be excited about learning. In doing so, librarians should strive to create a learning climate that supports not only the cognitive components of learning, but the social and affective components as well.

Here are a variety of strategies that librarians can use to increase motivation and engagement in learning:

- Promote summer reading programs to generate excitement about reading. Combine external motivators (e.g., points, prizes) with strategies designed to appeal to learners' inherent interests.
- Engage learners through projects and workshops that appeal to their curiosity and personal interests, such as art projects or family history research workshops. Offer a variety of project opportunities, as learners are often motivated by some subjects or topics but not others (e.g., math, space, bugs).
- Encourage learners to make, build, draw, and design things in the library that give them the opportunity to be creative and that they can share with family, friends, and others.

- Foster community partnerships to create opportunities for children and youth. Engage learners in projects that appeal to their innate desire to help others or make a difference in their communities. Provide opportunities for learners to share their work with community members.
- Provide places for clubs and community groups (e.g., mindfulness groups, gardening societies, art clubs) to meet to foster positive social relations and create a sense of belonging to increase learners' motivation and engagement.
- Promote use of games in the library to support learning.
- Make interactive learning materials and simulations available on library computers to engage learners' interests.
- Invite guests into the library to discuss projects that stimulate learners' curiosity (e.g., guest speakers who work in different professions and who come from different backgrounds may motivate learners to pursue certain hobbies or career goals).
- Provide positive feedback to learners about their efforts and projects to stimulate their innate desire to learn.

TEACHING LIBRARIAN'S CORNER

During instruction, librarians can use a variety of strategies to encourage learners to develop mastery goal orientations, cultivate implicit motivation, and understand the causes of past successes and failures. They can do this by designing tasks that are challenging and that appeal to learners' interests. They can also give learners some choice over their own learning, applaud their efforts, and help them to use strategies to set goals for themselves and recognize how to grow from past mistakes.

Librarians can use some of the following strategies to motivate learners during instruction:

- Ensure that tasks are suited to learners' abilities (i.e., not too difficult, not too easy) and that they are capable of succeeding at those tasks. Divide more difficult tasks into smaller chunks and provide adequate support.
- Keep learners engaged by designing tasks (or co-designing tasks with instructors) that are novel, surprising, varied, compelling, or relevant and that appeal to learners' curiosity, interests, or imaginations.
- Provide opportunities for individual work that allows learners to exert some control over the pace, focus, and goal of their own learning,

but be cautious about providing so many choices that they become overwhelming.

- Emphasize the inherent joys of learning and research and share your own personal enjoyment of these things. Place more emphasis on the process of learning and a spirit of inquiry than on "correct" answers.
- Provide prompt feedback to learners on their performance. Praise learners for their hard work to encourage an incremental view of intelligence. Teach learners that making mistakes is a part of learning.
- Help learners to understand the causes for their successes and failures, and offer specific and action-oriented feedback to help motivate them to improve. Avoid giving feedback that suggests that learners are less than competent (e.g., excessive praise for overly easy tasks).
- Avoid publicly announcing grades and be cautious about using too much social comparison.
- Be cautious and selective when using external rewards for learning.

FURTHER READING

Deci, Edward L., and Richard M. Ryan. *Intrinsic Motivation and Self-Determination in Human Behavior*. New York: Plenum, 1985.

Dweck, Carol S. *Self-Theories: Their Role in Motivation, Personality, and Development*. Philadelphia: Psychology, 1999.

Midgley, Carol, Eric M. Anderman, and Lynley H. Anderman. *Goals, Goal Structures, and Patterns of Adaptive Learning*. Mahwah, NJ: Taylor & Francis Group, 2002.

Weiner, Bernard. *An Attributional Theory of Motivation and Emotion*. New York: Springer-Verlag, 1986.

QUESTIONS TO CONSIDER

1. What is the relationship between a learner's view of intelligence and ability, and their goal orientations? How might these views manifest themselves during library instruction situations?

2. What role does the element of control play in motivating learners? How can librarians help learners feel that they are in control of their own learning?

3. What kinds of activities can be held in a library that might help to increase a learner's sense of self-determination?

NOTES

1. Dale Schunk, *Learning Theories: An Educational Perspective*, 8th ed. (New York: Pearson, 2019), 361; Eric M. Anderman and Christopher A. Wolters, "Goals, Values, and Affect: Influences on Student Motivation," in *Handbook of Educational Psychology*, ed. Patricia A. Alexander and Philip H. Winne, 2nd ed. (Mahwah, NJ: Routledge, 2006), 369–89.

2. Carole Ames, "Classrooms: Goals, Structures, and Student Motivation," *Journal of Educational Psychology* 84, no. 3 (1992): 261–71, https://doi.org/10.1037/0022-06 63.84.3.261; Carol S. Dweck, *Self-Theories: Their Role in Motivation, Personality, and Development* (Philadelphia: Psychology, 1999); Avi Kaplan et al., "Achievement Goals and Goal Structures," in *Goals, Goal Structures, and Patterns of Adaptive Learning*, ed. Carol Midgley, Eric M. Anderman, and Lynley H. Anderman (Mahwah, NJ: Taylor & Francis Group, 2002), 21–53.

3. Dweck, *Self-Theories*; Claudia M. Mueller and Carol S. Dweck, "Praise for Intelligence Can Undermine Children's Motivation and Performance," *Journal of Personality and Social Psychology* 75, no. 1 (July 1998): 33–52, https://doi.org/10.1037/0022-3514.75.1.33.

4. Kaplan et al., "Achievement Goals and Goal Structures."

5. Edward L. Deci, *The Psychology of Self-Determination* (Lexington, MA: Lexington Books, 1980); Edward L. Deci and Richard M. Ryan, *Intrinsic Motivation and Self-Determination in Human Behavior*, Perspectives in Social Psychology (New York: Plenum, 1985).

6. Deci, *The Psychology of Self-Determination*, 26.

7. Mihaly Csikszentmihalyi, *Flow: The Psychology of Optimal Experience* (New York: Harper & Row, 1990), 4.

8. Csikszentmihalyi, *Flow*; Mihaly Csikszentmihalyi and Jeanne Nakamura, "Dynamics of Intrinsic Motivation," in *Research on Motivation in Education*, ed. Russell Ames and Carole Ames, vol. 3, 3 vols. (Orlando, FL: Academic, 1984), 45–71.

9. Richard M. Ryan, James P. Connell, and Edward L. Deci, "A Motivational Analysis of Self-Determination and Self-Regulation in Education," in *Research on Motivation in Education*, ed. Russell Ames and Carole Ames, vol. 2, 3 vols. (Orlando, FL: Academic, 1984), 13–51; Edward L. Deci and Richard M. Ryan, "Self-Determination Theory of Motivation," in *Psychology of Classroom Learning: An Encyclopedia*, ed. Eric M. Anderman and Lynley H. Anderman, vol. 2, 2 vols. (Detroit: Gale Cengage Learning, 2009), 787–91.

10. Mark R. Lepper, David Greene, and Richard E. Nisbett, "Undermining Children's Intrinsic Interest with Extrinsic Reward: A Test of the 'Overjustification' Hypothesis," *Journal of Personality and Social Psychology* 28, no. 1 (October 1973): 129–37, https://doi.org/10.1037/h0035519; Deci, *The Psychology of Self-Determination*, 35–38.

11. Bernard Weiner, "An Attributional Theory of Achievement Motivation and Emotion," *Psychological Review* 92, no. 4 (1985): 548–73, https://doi.org/10.1037/0033-295X.92.4.548; Bernard Weiner, *Human Motivation: Metaphors, Theories, and Research* (Newbury Park, CA: Sage, 1992); Bernard Weiner, *An Attributional Theory of Motivation and Emotion* (New York: Springer-Verlag, 1986).

12. Schunk, *Learning Theories*, 383; Sandra Graham and Bernard Weiner, "Theories and Principles of Motivation," in *Handbook of Educational Psychology*, ed. David C. Berliner and Robert C. Calfee (New York: Routledge, 1996), 63–84.

13. Weiner, "An Attributional Theory of Achievement Motivation and Emotion"; Weiner, *An Attributional Theory of Motivation and Emotion*; Weiner, *Human Motivation*.

8

AFFECT

THEORETICAL OVERVIEW

Learners may be excited or bored by the subjects they are studying. They might feel inspired by teachers or frustrated by assignments. They might enjoy the social context of the classroom or feel embarrassed in front of other students. No matter what the situation, learning is an emotional process.

Using the library can also be an emotional experience for many learners. Learners may discover information that makes them excited to learn, or they may feel intimidated by the size of the library, the organization of books, the technologies available, or the difficulty of reading challenging material.

While affect has the potential to detract from learning, it may also help people to become more engaged in the learning process. It plays a significant role in the quality of learning and has a strong influence on learners' attention, motivation, and persistence in the face of difficulties. The role of affect in learning can best be understood with attention to its role in information processing, its relation to motivation, and the necessity for emotion regulation.

Affect and Information Processing

Affect is a broad category that includes both emotions and moods. *Emotions* are complex responses to specific stimuli, which can be either external (e.g., difficulty using technology) or internal (e.g., ruminations about writing a lengthy research paper) that are experienced in relation to a goal. A person experiencing an emotion may not be consciously aware of what caused it. In comparison to emotions, *moods* lack a specific cause or object of focus. Emotions may be shorter-lived and more intense, while moods may be longer-lived and less intense.[1] The experience of affect can be influenced by several elements, such as a learner's personality traits, their attitudes toward learning, their cultural influences, and their learning preferences.[2]

The term *emotions* is often used interchangeably with *feelings*, but emotions include a feeling response as well as a whole body response that may prompt action. Emotions consist of several components, as described below, with examples of a student who must give a presentation in front of a class:

- a subjective feeling (e.g., "I feel anxious")
- a physiological element (e.g., flushed cheeks)
- an appraisal element through which the person makes sense of the emotion and situation (e.g., "I am a bad public speaker")
- a motivational or action tendency, which may or may not be carried out (e.g., a desire to skip class to avoid having to give the presentation)
- a motor activity that expresses what a person is feeling (e.g., playing with hands in an expression of nervousness)[3]

Each of these components may influence the others. Specifically, a learner may experience emotions in response to their continued appraisals of situations, which may in turn result in sustaining or changing the emotional response. The student described above may appraise their performance during the class presentation as going better or worse than expected, which may trigger an intensified, diminished, or different emotional response. Similarly, the student may change their motor activities by ceasing to play with their hands, standing up straight, and smiling, which may in turn make them feel more confident.

In educational settings, learners constantly experience a variety of affective states that may either assist with or detract from their learning. Reinhard Pekrun has described several ways in which emotions can be classified in academic contexts:

- *Positive or negative:* For example, a learner may experience pleasant or unpleasant emotions (e.g., excitement or dread) in response to a learning activity.
- *Activating or deactivating:* For example, a learner who is excited about a topic of research may be more inclined to take action, such as finding relevant sources, while a learner who is bored may be less inclined to take action.

- *Activity- or outcome-focused:* For example, a learner may feel interest when participating in activities such as completing a math problem or learning about astronomy, or feel disappointed by the outcome of an academic endeavor, such as receiving a bad grade on a test. Outcome emotions can be either forward- or backward-looking; for example, a learner might feel pride in having done well on a research paper or feel anxious about a looming assignment deadline.[4]

In addition to experiencing emotional responses in relation to learning tasks and subjects, learners experience emotions regarding the educational and social settings in which learning occurs. Learners may feel intimidated by other students, confused by the instructions given in class, or encouraged by the feedback they receive about their assignments. Certain features of instruction may also prompt certain emotions in learners. When learners are given more autonomy during the learning process, for instance, they may experience positive emotional engagement. Similarly, when librarians and other educators convey their own positive emotions, learners may experience positive emotions as well.

The experience of affect plays an important role in the way a person processes information. From an evolutionary perspective, fear or anger has prompted defensive responses to threats, sadness has provoked an inward focus and reevaluation of situations, and interest or excitement has prompted people to explore their environments or connect with others.[5] These fundamental affective responses also apply to learning environments.

During the learning process, emotions influence attention and recall. If learners' emotions are focused on friends or text messages, then they may be distracted from learning. Positive emotions such as interest or curiosity may help learners to focus on and remember content, even if that content is difficult. On the other hand, strong negative emotions may inhibit learners from focusing their attention or remembering information, as they use cognitive resources to attempt to cope with or expel their bad feelings.

While positive emotions may improve learning and negative emotions detract from it, this is not always the case. To illustrate, learners are more likely to attend to and remember positive information if they are in a positive mood and negative information if they are in a negative mood.[6] Certain affective states may also influence different types of learning. Positive affect can lead to the use of creative, flexible, and open-minded approaches to problem-solving, as positive feelings indicate the absence of threat. At the same time, negative affective states may assist with greater attention to detail and more careful analysis.[7]

Moreover, learners may mistake their feelings about a subject as information about that subject, an idea known as *affect-as-information*.[8] When learners use their affective states as information, their learning may be hindered and their judgments biased. For example, a learner who has strong negative feelings about a book may resist learning the positive lessons it has to teach. They may even believe that their feelings, rather than reasoned arguments, justify banning the book.

The Emotional Aspects of False Information

Librarians can help to make learners aware of the role that emotions play in making people more susceptible to believing inaccurate information. False information frequently engages readers and viewers on an emotional level, appealing to their feelings of approval or outrage. Much inaccurate information is shared through social media posts, which makes it increasingly easy for learners to stay in their own information bubbles, avoiding exposure to different ideas while confirming their own opinions and beliefs. This encourages learners to become strongly and often emotionally attached to their current ways of thinking, even if those are incorrect. The overwhelming amount of false information on the internet, as well as the increasing sophistication with which it is presented, also makes it more seductive and encourages rapid, emotional responses.

Emotion and Motivation

Learners are engaged in a continual process of appraisal of learning tasks to determine whether those tasks are consistent with or threatening to their personal goals, interests, and well-being. If the former, then they may experience positive emotions that promote engagement; if the latter, then they may experience negative emotions that promote disengagement.

The relationship between emotions and the motivation to learn is often complex. In educational settings, emotions play a significant role in learners' motivation to engage in or refrain from the pursuit of academic goals. While positive, activating emotions often aid the learning process, this is not always the case. Negative emotions such as anxiety may prompt a learner to study harder (although too much anxiety can be inhibiting), while positive emotions such as assurance may prompt a learner to study less. Similarly, an activating emotion such as curiosity may inspire a learner to engage in learning, but an activating emotion such as overconfidence may prompt a learner to disengage.

Learners' emotions are also strongly influenced by both the value they place on a subject or activity and their perceived control over their actions, an idea described by Pekrun's *control-value theory* of emotion.[9] For instance, a learner who values solving a math problem, writing a short story, or designing a science experiment, and who feels that these activities are important, will probably be motivated to engage in these tasks. Similarly, if the learner also perceives that they have control over their ability to do well in math, writing, or science, then they may also be more likely to engage in those activities. If learners do not value or feel control over certain academic tasks, then they may experience a feeling of disinterest or boredom.

Emotions also factor into learners' assessments of the causes of their past academic successes and failures, which influence their motivation to engage in related activities in the future. This process of searching for the causes of particular outcomes and its effect on future behaviors is described by *attribution theory*.[10] When learners succeed or fail at a task, they may feel positive or negative emotions, which prompt them to look for a cause. These causes can be located in three dimensions: *locus* (internal or external to the learner), *stability* (constant or varying over time and situations), and *controllability* (see chapter 7, "Motivation").

A learner's causal assessment and the accompanying dimensions further influence their emotional response to the success or failure, which in turn influences their subsequent motivation. For example, if a learner succeeds at a task, they may feel a sense of pride if they determine that the reason for their success was their hard work, a cause which is internal, unstable, and controllable. This feeling of pride may motivate them to continue working hard in the future. But if a learner fails at a task, they may feel shame if they determine that the reason was their ability, a cause which is internal, stable, and uncontrollable. This feeling of shame may discourage them from trying in the future.

The feelings that accompany these causal attributions, particularly the dimension of control, may influence a learner's self-efficacy, or their belief in their ability to execute certain tasks in order to achieve certain outcomes (see chapter 5, "Observation"). A learner's pride in academic success enhances their self-esteem and increases their feelings of confidence about the chance of future successes, thereby increasing their motivation. On the other hand, feelings of shame about an academic failure may lead to a lack of confidence, decreased self-esteem, a sense of hopelessness, and a fear of future failure, thereby decreasing their motivation. While a learner may feel relief if they believe that their success was the result of luck, they may not feel that they have control over their ability to replicate this success in the future, resulting in a lack of increased motivation.

Emotion Regulation

Learning to regulate emotions is particularly important in educational contexts. *Emotion regulation* refers to the ability to understand and manage one's emotions to facilitate goal-seeking and healthy social relationships.[11]

Emotion regulation involves three components: the engagement of a goal to alter the emotion, the use of an emotion regulation strategy, and the consequences of that strategy.[12] This process may or may not occur in a conscious manner. Attempts to employ strategies to regulate emotions may occur at several different points in the experience. While emotion regulation may involve attempts to manage the

TABLE 8.1

Emotion regulation strategies and examples

EMOTION REGULATION STRATEGY	DESCRIPTION	EXAMPLE
Situation selection	Choosing to engage in or avoid certain situations that elicit particular emotional responses	Putting one's cell phone on "do not disturb" to avoid emotional distractions while studying
Situation modification	Modifying a situation after it has already begun in order to influence one's emotional response	Moving to a different seat in the library to avoid becoming frustrated by the talking of people seated nearby
Attentional deployment	Choosing where to direct one's attention in order to influence emotions	Distracting oneself from feeling nervous about an end-of-semester assignment by thinking about summer vacation
Cognitive change	Using strategies to reevaluate a situation in order to change an emotional response	Reappraising an anxiety-inducing research assignment as an opportunity to learn more about an interesting topic
Response modulation	Changing how one expresses or responds to an emotion after it has already begun to be felt	Engaging in deep breathing to calm oneself when feeling nervous about speaking in front of a group

Table compiled from concepts found in James J. Gross, "The Emerging Field of Emotion Regulation: An Integrative Review," *Review of General Psychology* 2, no. 3 (1998): 271–99.

emotions of both oneself and others, self-regulation is the focus of the examples used in table 8.1.

Finally, emotional regulation is often addressed through programs that promote *emotional intelligence*, which includes skills related to understanding and regulating emotions, recognizing emotions in others, and understanding the connections between emotions and thinking.[13] *Social and emotional learning*—which includes instruction in self-awareness, self-management, social awareness, relationship skills, and responsible decision-making—is one approach to teaching emotional intelligence at the K–12 level.[14]

IMPLICATIONS FOR LIBRARIES

Using the library and its resources can sometimes be an anxious and uncertain experience for many younger or inexperienced learners. Anxiety, the uneasy feeling of anticipation of a future misfortune, is one of the most commonly studied emotions in academic contexts.[15] Test anxiety and math anxiety are two of the most frequent subjects of exploration, but library anxiety has been frequently studied as well. First explained by Constance Mellon in 1986 in a study of university students, *library anxiety* describes learners' fear and anxiety about not knowing how to navigate the physical library or how to conduct research.[16] While the information age has considerably changed the nature of library research since Mellon first published her study, library anxiety continues to be a common experience for many inexperienced library users.

Here are a variety of strategies that librarians can use to ensure that learners have positive emotional experiences when using the library for learning:

- Host welcoming activities to get learners comfortable with the library setting. Offer library tours, open houses, or demos of library spaces, equipment, and resources.
- Provide events and activities that generate positive emotions (e.g., curiosity, interest, excitement) in learners, and give learners opportunities to share work that they are proud of.
- Invite school, community, and campus groups to hold events or meetups in the library that give participants a sense of belonging and that generate school or community pride.
- Ensure that help services are easily accessible. Encourage learners to ask for help when they need it. Provide peer assistance for those learners who may feel more comfortable with getting help in this manner.

- Offer a variety of training sessions to help learners feel comfortable using technologies.
- Provide self-service information about library resources for learners who feel more comfortable finding their own answers, such as "do it yourself" web pages, library maps, handouts, and video explanations.
- Explain the phenomenon of "library anxiety" to educators and help them understand that library instruction can help to reduce or prevent library anxiety.
- Make personal connections to learners and interact with learners outside of the library setting and in informal contexts.
- Show that librarians and library staff are caring, warm, and approachable.

....

Emotional Labor

Librarians who engage frequently with the public may feel the effects of *emotional labor*, which J. Andrew Morris and Daniel C. Feldman define as "the effort, planning, and control needed to express organizationally desired emotion during interpersonal transactions."[17] Morris and Feldman describe how the extent of emotional labor that one experiences is affected by the frequency, variety, duration, and intensity of emotions needing to be expressed, as well as the dissonance that may exist between what one is feeling and what one must display. Too much emotional labor can result in exhaustion and burnout, so librarians should engage in frequent reflection about their emotional interactions, strive for greater self-awareness, set boundaries when necessary, and seek emotional support to avoid feeling the negative effects of emotional labor.

....

TEACHING LIBRARIAN'S CORNER

To respond to the affective component of learning during instruction situations, librarians should combine appropriately challenging tasks with emotional support strategies such as encouraging persistence, using humor, and acknowledging and addressing emotions. Tasks should be challenging enough to stimulate learners, thereby generating interest and excitement, without being so challenging that they generate confusion and frustration. Tasks that are too easy may lead to boredom.

In addition, the emotions librarians convey while teaching may have a significant impact on the emotions of learners. When librarians exhibit positive emotions that convey enjoyment and enthusiasm, learners are more likely to experience their own positive emotions that increase their motivation to learn.

Librarians can use some of the following strategies to address the affective components of learning during instruction:

- Engage with learners regarding their interests. Probe by asking questions about their connections to topics and ideas to engage positive emotions. Encourage learners to pursue inquiry projects about topics that they are passionate about.
- Ask learners to establish and reflect upon their own goals for learning to engage positive attitudes.
- Provide clear instructions and examples for tasks and assignments to ensure that learners do not experience confusion.
- Avoid too much lecturing, and keep instruction varied and active so that learners do not experience boredom.
- Provide opportunities for learners who enjoy social learning to work with their peers, but keep in mind that learners who dislike social learning may experience negative emotions during group work.
- Use humor, when appropriate, to generate positive emotions in the classroom.
- Acknowledge learners' emotions or potentially emotion-inducing situations. If appropriate, share your own honest emotions (e.g., frustration, discomfort, excitement) about your experiences engaging with similar tasks (e.g., your own research projects or craft projects).
- Teach strategies that learners can use to regulate their own emotions during learning (e.g., help learners to anticipate frustrating parts of the research process and offer strategies to work through this). Help learners to understand the causes of their successes and failures and offer them strategies for improvement.
- Convey positive emotions during instruction, but avoid overdoing it. Use strategies to regulate your own emotions in classroom contexts (e.g., take deep breaths when frustrated, reappraise difficult situations, moderate your expectations).

FURTHER READING

Goetz, Thomas, and Nathan C. Hall. *Emotion, Motivation, and Self-Regulation: A Handbook for Teachers*. Bingley, UK: Emerald Group, 2013.

Pekrun, Reinhard, and Lisa Linnenbrink-Garcia, eds. *International Handbook of Emotions in Education*. New York: Routledge, 2014.

Schutz, Paul A., and Reinhard Pekrun, eds. *Emotion in Education*. Amsterdam: Academic, 2007.

QUESTIONS TO CONSIDER

1. How might library anxiety exhibit itself in library users? What strategies can librarians use to help mitigate these feelings in learners?

2. Select a common emotion that learners experience (e.g., pride, embarrassment, confidence, frustration, confusion, boredom, excitement, anger, interest). How might this emotion be addressed through library services or library instruction? Provide some different examples.

3. What are some strategies that librarians can use to teach learners how to become aware of and monitor their own emotional engagement when accessing information online?

NOTES

1. Reinhard Pekrun and Lisa Linnenbrink-Garcia, "Introduction to Emotions in Education," in *International Handbook of Emotions in Education*, ed. Reinhard Pekrun and Lisa Linnenbrink-Garcia (New York: Routledge, 2014), 1–10, https://doi.org/10.4324/9780203148211.

2. Vera Schuman and Klaus R. Scherer, "Concepts and Structures of Emotion," in *International Handbook of Emotions in Education*, ed. Reinhard Pekrun and Lisa Linnenbrink-Garcia (New York: Routledge, 2014), 13–35, https://doi.org/10.4324/9780203148211.

3. Tina Hascher, "Learning and Emotion: Perspectives for Theory and Research," *European Educational Research Journal* 9, no. 1 (2010): 13–28, https://doi.org/10.2304/eerj.2010.9.1.13; Schuman and Scherer, "Concepts and Structures of Emotion."

4. Reinhard Pekrun, "Academic Emotions," in *Handbook of Motivation at School*, ed. Kathryn R. Wentzel and David B. Miele, 2nd ed. (New York: Routledge, 2016), 120–44.

5. Julia A. Harris and Derek Isaacowitz, "Emotion in Cognition," in *International Encyclopedia of the Social & Behavioral Sciences*, ed. James D. Wright, 2nd ed. (Oxford: Elsevier, 2015), 461–66, https://doi.org/10.1016/B978-0-08-097086-8.25003-4.

6. Joseph P. Forgas, "Introduction: The Role of Affect in Social Cognition," in *Feeling and Thinking: The Role of Affect in Social Cognition*, ed. Joseph P. Forgas (Cambridge: Cambridge University Press, 2000), 1–28.

7. Harris and Isaacowitz, "Emotion in Cognition."

8. Forgas, "Introduction: The Role of Affect in Social Cognition."

9. Reinhard Pekrun and Raymond P. Perry, "Control-Value Theory of Achievement Emotion," in *International Handbook of Emotions in Education*, ed. Reinhard Pekrun and Lisa Linnenbrink-Garcia (New York: Routledge, 2014), 120–41, https://doi.org/10.4324/9780203148211.

10. Sandra Graham and April Z. Taylor, "An Attributional Approach to Emotional Life in the Classroom," in *International Handbook of Emotions in Education*, ed. Reinhard Pekrun and Lisa Linnenbrink-Garcia (New York: Routledge, 2014), 96–119, https://doi.org/10.4324/9780203148211; Bernard Weiner, "An Attributional Theory of Achievement Motivation and Emotion," *Psychological Review* 92, no. 4 (1985): 548–73, https://doi.org/10.1037/0033-295X.92.4.548.

11. Monique Boekaerts, "Emotions, Emotion Regulation, and Self-Regulation of Learning," in *Handbook of Self-Regulation of Learning and Performance*, ed. Dale H. Schunk and Barry Zimmerman (New York: Routledge, 2011), 408–25.

12. James J. Gross, "Emotion Regulation: Conceptual and Empirical Foundations," in *Handbook of Emotion Regulation*, ed. James J. Gross (New York: Guilford, 2013), 3–20.

13. Veleka Allen et al., "Emotional Intelligence in Education: From Pop to Emerging Science," in *International Handbook of Emotions in Education*, ed. Reinhard Pekrun and Lisa Linnenbrink-Garcia (New York: Routledge, 2014), 162–82, https://doi.org/10.4324/9780203148211.

14. "Fundamentals of SEL," CASEL, https://casel.org/fundamentals-of-sel/.

15. Carolyn Jackson, "Affective Dimensions of Learning," in *Contemporary Theories of Learning: Learning Theorists . . . in Their Own Words*, ed. Knud Illeris, 2nd ed. (New York: Routledge, 2018), 139–52.

16. Constance A. Mellon, "Library Anxiety: A Grounded Theory and Its Development," *College & Research Libraries* 76, no. 3 (2015): 276–82, https://doi.org/10.5860/crl.76.3.276.

17. J. Andrew Morris and Daniel C. Feldman, "The Dimensions, Antecedents, and Consequences of Emotional Labor," *The Academy of Management Review* 21, no. 4 (1996): 986–1010, https://doi.org/10.2307/259161.

9

CONTEXT

THEORETICAL OVERVIEW

Context matters for learning. This is the notion behind the theory of *situated learning*, which holds that learning is intricately connected to the physical and social contexts in which it takes place.[1] Situations, and the activities that occur within them, have an impact on the ways that knowledge and skills are acquired. Situated learning has implications for the teaching of library, research, and other skills, and librarians can play important roles in creating and facilitating the contexts in which learning occurs.

Situated learning theory, which gained increased attention in the late 1980s and early 1990s, raises issues about the importance of context for the retrieval of information and the transfer of skills to other settings. One specific approach to situated learning theory—communities of practice—has emphasized the role that communities and participation play in learning.

Situated Learning

Situated learning theorists advocate that educators consider the role of context when designing instructional situations to better help people learn. As support for this notion, they point to the ways that many concepts evolve within the contexts of activities and practices. Learning a language provides a good example. Because people's understanding of language is affected by the context in which it is produced, and because the meaning of words is constantly evolving in practice, language is learned most effectively within situational contexts.[2]

An important component of learning new information is being able to retrieve it for later use and apply it to new situations. Learning within contexts can help people better remember information and understand how to retrieve information that is relevant to particular situations. This ability to apply knowledge and skills is apparent in the behaviors of experts in a particular field. Experts possess knowledge and skills that are contextualized; in other words, when faced with particular contexts, they know how to retrieve the relevant knowledge and skills from memory to accomplish a task.[3]

When learners learn concepts that are completely divorced from context, they may have trouble understanding how to apply them. In traditional classrooms, students often learn concepts in the abstract, which may make it difficult to know how to transfer what they learn to real-world situations. While some educators have argued that learning abstract concepts allows for transferal to a variety of situations, situated learning theorists suggest that presenting concepts in too abstract a manner can make learning difficult. For example, students may learn a variety of statistical processes in a mathematics class but be unable to apply them when given a set of real-world data. However, some learning theorists have also noted that the connection between transferability and the learning context is dependent on what is being learned. Skills such as reading, for instance, are less context-dependent and transfer easily to a variety of situations.[4] In many cases, the learning of concepts in the abstract can be combined with learning them in situational contexts.

Proponents of situated learning also argue that knowledge is best learned within *authentic contexts*, which are situations and activities that are drawn from real-life situations. Learning through authentic contexts involves the incorporation of physical settings outside of the classroom, collaborative engagement, modeling by experts, and access to multiple perspectives.[5] *Service-learning* is one type of authentic learning experience that enables learners to participate in community service activities that allow them to apply their knowledge and skills to real-world situations.

Even when instruction is confined to the classroom environment, however, librarians and other educators can still employ a real-world approach. As an example, one method of instruction that is common in business courses is the use of case studies; these are company scenarios that challenge learners to identify problems, apply strategies, and design solutions to issues related to management, marketing, business ethics, and others. In medical education, learners are often required to work through clinical cases as if they were doctors helping patients, a process that requires them to identify medical problems and develop hypotheses about how to treat them.

While situated learning is important, providing instruction that is over-contextualized may also make it difficult for learners to apply what they learn to new contexts. Therefore, it can be useful for librarians and other educators to provide multiple contexts and examples when teaching skills so that learners can gain repeated practice applying and transferring what they have learned. Librarians and other educators can also engage learners in "what if" scenarios in which different features of case studies are altered, or they can ask learners to examine iterations of similar cases to practice applying processes and concepts.[6]

Communities of Practice

Not only is context important in situated learning theory, but the concepts of community and participation are critical as well. One approach to situated learning that emphasizes these elements is that of communities of practice, developed by Jean Lave, an anthropologist who studied traditional apprenticeship practices among tailors in West Africa, and Etienne Wenger, an educational theorist. Lave observed that apprentices learn a craft not necessarily through direct instruction (i.e., explicit teaching of content) but through their participation in specific social configurations. Lave and Wenger called these social configurations communities of practice, which are comprised of people who "engage in a process of collective learning in a shared domain of human endeavor."[7] While employment situations such as the tailoring practices studied by Lave are examples of communities of practice, the latter can also include different kinds of everyday situations in which people participate, such as sports teams, religious congregations, and clubs.

Lave and Wenger did not view knowledge as consisting solely of pieces of abstract information to be acquired. Rather, knowledge results from active participation and engagement in meaningful activities. Thus, learning and activity are intimately related. Learning is not something that happens only in formal classroom settings or through direct instruction, but it is instead "an integral part of our everyday lives" that occurs through social engagement in meaningful activities.[8]

Learning through participation is about more than just taking part in activities; it involves joining in the practices of certain communities and engaging in the construction and negotiation of meaning within those communities. *Practices* consist of the discourses, methods, and skills used within a community. Meaning is often given shape through a community's *artifacts*, the "tools, symbols, stories, terms, and concepts" that become accepted parts of its practice.[9] This process of giving concrete form to more abstract components of a practice is known as *reification*.[10]

For librarians, artifacts of practice might include cataloging standards and records, information literacy documents, library guides, library databases, and the specialized vocabulary used to describe search tools and processes.

A core concept underpinning the theory of communities of practice is the notion of *legitimate peripheral participation*, which describes a learner's movement from partial to full participation within a community (see figure 9.1).[11] The concept of legitimate peripheral participation can be understood through the practice of apprenticeship. Lave and Wenger described how apprentices move from peripheral to full participation within their communities of practice:

> Apprentices gradually assemble a general idea of what constitutes the practice of the community. This . . . might include who is involved; what they do; what everyday life is like; how masters talk, walk, work, and generally conduct their lives; how people who are not part of the community of practice interact with it; what other learners are doing; and what learners need to learn to become full practitioners.[12]

When newcomers join a community of practice, they participate only marginally at first. Novices begin by performing simple activities but gradually take on more complex ones through their participation in the community. As they observe the activities of others and practice those skills, they become more adept and are able to participate more fully. Thus, participation becomes a way of learning. Eventually, the newcomers become "old-timers" and the community of practice sustains itself through the incorporation of new members over time.

Through their increased participation in their communities of practice, learners in turn influence and shape the activities of the community. Learners join other members in co-creating activities, and all members bring about changes in their environment. Through learners' contributions to their communities, they may potentially change communal knowledge and practices. Not only do individuals learn, but all members learn together. Knowledge itself is located within the community, rather than in an individual. In fact, "communities of practice can be thought of as shared histories of learning."[13]

Over time, people's participation in a community of practice becomes not just a means of and a motivation for learning, but also an important part of their identity. People join many different communities of practice throughout their lives through the jobs they work, the schools they attend, and the social activities and hobbies they engage in. Wenger described how "we all belong to many communities of

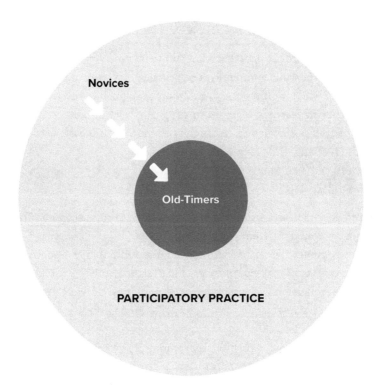

FIGURE 9.1

The movement of novice learners from partial to full participation in a community through legitimate peripheral participation

practice: some past, some current; some as full members, some in more peripheral ways. Some may be central to our identities while others are more incidental."[14] All of these communities provide different opportunities for learning.

The theory of communities of practice underscores the notion that learning does not necessarily require formal teaching, and in fact, very often occurs in settings outside of educational institutions and structured learning environments. Communities of practice often develop organically, but they can also be formed with an intent to promote learning. As an example, library administrators and managers can encourage the development of communities of practice in their organizations as a way of improving staff knowledge and skills to further their missions and adjust to changing circumstances.

IMPLICATIONS FOR LIBRARIES

Libraries are critical for supporting local communities of practice and helping to situate learning. Existing communities of practice may seek out library spaces as meeting places, while in other cases, librarians may form their own communities of practice to bring learners together in support of shared interests. In addition, librarians are well-positioned to create the community connections that allow for the generation of authentic learning experiences.

Librarians can use some of the following strategies to support situated approaches to learning:

- Form in-person and online themed book clubs to create communities of practice around different topics of interest.
- Form communities of practice centered around library resources and services, such as making, robotics, and design.
- Provide collections that support the activities of local community groups and invite participants to provide input into the development of these collections.
- Advertise the library as a space for community groups to meet, and provide adequate technical support for these groups.
- Create and promote lists of local place-based resources for learning and sites for virtual field trips.
- Collaborate with community groups, such as outdoor or gardening groups, to sponsor authentic learning experiences in the library or at off-site locations.
- Collaborate with community groups to promote service-learning opportunities for children and youth, and facilitate discussion sessions that enable learners to reflect upon and share what they learned through service.
- Invite learners of different ages to intern in the library.
- Provide spaces or events in the library to celebrate the activities of local community groups.

TEACHING LIBRARIAN'S CORNER

When using a situational learning approach, librarians should attempt to relate classroom learning to real-life contexts whenever possible. Understanding basic perspectives, methods, and tasks that are common in particular disciplines can be helpful when situating information literacy instruction. In addition, collaborations with other educators and community members can also help librarians to devise situated learning opportunities.

Librarians can use some of the following strategies to incorporate situated learning theory into their teaching:

- Have conversations with other educators to better understand the ways that they view and practice information literacy skills within the context of their disciplines.
- Review disciplinary documents, such as textbooks, trade publications, accreditation standards, and other sources to better understand the situations in which information literacy skills are needed.
- Co-design assignments with educators to ensure that information literacy instruction is situated in real-life and disciplinary contexts.
- Introduce case studies to situate the teaching of information literacy skills. Ask learners to identify the problem that each case poses, strategize about ways to obtain information about it, and research possible solutions.
- Incorporate local problems that relate to learners' own lives, and provide learners with some resources for local investigation. Collaborate with school and community partners to identify these local problems. For example, librarians can use examples of problems in their own cities or towns (such as issues with homelessness or fire safety) and have learners research the situations and generate possible solutions.
- Take learners on fields trips in the campus or community, or ask learners to interview local experts. Create assignments that integrate these trips or interviews.
- Bring learners to visit an archives to see physical examples of historical manuscripts and artifacts and learn specific strategies for how to use primary sources to complete a project.

Using Case Studies in Library Instruction

Librarians can use case studies to situate the teaching of information literacy skills. For example, an academic librarian might give any of three different multi-paragraph case studies to small groups of education students, and ask them to position themselves as educational consultants tasked with helping current teachers. The cases might describe (1) a teacher having a disciplinary situation with a secondary student, (2) a teacher helping an elementary student who is struggling with reading skills, and (3) a teacher

(continued)

who has been instructed to implement a new math curriculum. The librarian teaches the education students relevant information literacy skills and then asks them to use each scenario to (1) determine which types of information sources would be most useful for addressing the teacher's situation, (2) find and review sources to determine possible approaches, and (3) make a plan for how to share what they find with the teacher they are assisting.

FURTHER READING

Herrington, Tony, and Jan Herrington. *Authentic Learning Environments in Higher Education*. Hershey, PA: Information Science, 2005.

Wenger, Etienne. *Communities of Practice: Learning, Meaning, and Identity*. Cambridge: Cambridge University Press, 1998.

Wenger, Etienne, Richard A. McDermott, and William Snyder. *Cultivating Communities of Practice: A Guide to Managing Knowledge*. Boston: Harvard Business Review Press, 2002.

QUESTIONS TO CONSIDER

1. Pick a particular social context or academic discipline. What strategies might a librarian use to situate the learning of an information literacy or other skill within that social context or discipline?

2. What school, campus, or community collaborations can librarians engage in to capitalize on the notion that learning frequently occurs within communities of practice?

3. What is the significance of legitimate peripheral participation for learning? How might librarians use communities of practice to enhance their own learning or the learning of newer library staff and interns?

NOTES

1. Dale Schunk, *Learning Theories: An Educational Perspective*, 8th ed. (New York: Pearson, 2019), 317.

2. John Seely Brown, Allan Collins, and Paul Duguid, "Situated Cognition and the Culture of Learning," *Educational Researcher* 18, no. 1 (January 1, 1989): 32–42, https://doi.org/10.3102/0013189X018001032.

3. John Bransford et al., *How People Learn: Brain, Mind, Experience, and School* (Washington, DC: National Academy, 1999), 31.

4. John R. Anderson, Lynne M. Reder, and Herbert A. Simon, "Situated Learning and Education," *Educational Researcher* 25, no. 4 (1996): 5–11, https://doi.org/10.2307/1176775.

5. Tony Herrington and Jan Herrington, *Authentic Learning Environments in Higher Education* (Hershey, PA: Information Science, 2005), 1–13.

6. Bransford et al., *How People Learn*, 50–51.

7. Etienne Wenger and Beverly Wenger-Trayner, "Communities of Practice: A Brief Introduction," April 15, 2015, www.wenger-trayner.com/introduction-to-communities-of-practice/.

8. Etienne Wenger, *Communities of Practice: Learning, Meaning, and Identity* (Cambridge: Cambridge University Press, 1998), 8.

9. Wenger, *Communities of Practice*, 59.

10. Wenger, *Communities of Practice*, 58–59.

11. Jean Lave and Etienne Wenger, *Situated Learning: Legitimate Peripheral Participation* (Cambridge: Cambridge University Press, 1991), 29.

12. Lave and Wenger, *Situated Learning*, 95.

13. Wenger, *Communities of Practice*, 86.

14. Wenger, *Communities of Practice*, 158.

DIALOGUE

THEORETICAL OVERVIEW

Dialogue has long been used as a teaching and learning strategy. Over two thousand years ago, Plato described how Socrates asked questions of his followers in order to help them use reason to explore complex ethical issues. In the universities of Europe during the Middle Ages, students learned by engaging in *disputatio*, or disputation, whereby they used reason and argumentation to debate questions under the guidance of a teacher. Today dialogue is still one of the best ways that people can learn from each other.

Not only do people learn through face-to-face dialogue, but today's learners are also engaged in a kind of dialogue with the abundance of information sources that they ingest daily through the internet and other media. In using the internet, learners must constantly use critical thinking skills to recognize persuasive or deceptive messages to ensure that the information they are using to make decisions is reliable and accurate.

Librarians have an important role to play in promoting healthy dialogues within their communities and in teaching the kinds of critical thinking skills that enable learners to discern meaning in information sources and construct good arguments of their own.

Dialogical Thinking

Dialogue describes a type of communication in which participants engage with others in a continuous exchange with the goal of arriving at new or deeper understandings.[1]

While dialogues are often focused on specific issues or questions, they may unfold in a manner unknown to the participants, who take an open-minded attitude toward the possibilities of learning from the interaction.

Learning through dialogue supports a constructivist view of learning whereby learners encounter new perspectives through exchanges with others, and this dialogue prompts them to assimilate and accommodate this information to achieve new understandings (see chapter 1, "Constructing Knowledge"). Learning through dialogue is also an essential component of Vygotsky's description of the social context of learning, through which knowledge is socially constructed and shared through language.[2] Vygotsky described how internalized speech provides the form and structure that enables higher-level thinking, and written communication or oral dialogue with others becomes a means of developing and shaping learners' nascent, internal ideas. In addition, he also described how the zone of proximal development provides a way for children to stretch to new capabilities by engaging in dialogue with a more knowledgeable member of society (see chapter 2, "Collaboration"; and chapter 13, "Guidance").

When learners engage in dialogue, they are using *dialogical thinking*, which involves exploring different points of view in order to improve one's own thinking about issues.[3] Dialogical thinking helps people learn by:

- improving their knowledge about the subjects being discussed
- sharpening their reasoning and critical thinking skills
- increasing their metacognitive awareness
- developing a greater appreciation for diverse points of view

Dialogical thinking forces learners to think through various facets of complex issues in ways that allow for deeper understanding. Through engaging in dialogue about different issues, learners practice using a variety of advanced thinking skills, including defining, comparing, contrasting, questioning assumptions, examining evidence, selecting relevant information, breaking down wholes into parts, adjusting strategies, and thinking through implications. Finally, dialogical thinking provides practice in thinking through the kinds of complex problems and thorny issues that learners encounter in the real world—problems and issues that can only be fully understood when considering multiple points of view.

Dialogical thinking also involves being aware of and closely examining one's own perspectives, assumptions, and biases—which learners are often unconscious of—in order to ensure that these do not prevent them from fully and honestly exploring issues. Through dialogical thinking and discourse with others, learners can practice examining their own points of view, uncovering their assumptions and inconsistencies, clarifying their own thinking, and constructing rational arguments to support their opinions.

Learning through dialogue includes an attitudinal component as well. Dialogical thinking involves a commitment on the part of participants to engage with other people in a manner that is open-minded, respectful, and committed to mutual understanding. It also requires empathy; in other words, learners must put themselves in others' shoes and imagine life from their perspectives. This dispositional aspect is part of what often makes dialogue distinct from debate. With dialogue, participants are interested in listening and learning from each other, exploring multiple perspectives, changing their own points of view when appropriate, and achieving consensus. In debate, by contrast, participants may be more interested in winning the argument than expanding their understanding of a topic or changing their perspective. When learners are genuinely committed to open exchange, dialogue can provide an excellent means of understanding differences among people.

While it is not easy to facilitate good dialogue, librarians and other educators can use a variety of methods to foster strong thinking skills, respectful communication, and open-minded attitudes. First, they must emphasize that dialogical thinking involves moving beyond learners' personal preferences or opinions. Instead, learners should use reason to arrive at better judgments after thoroughly understanding all sides of an issue.[4] Second, librarians and other educators should teach that dialogical thinking involves being committed to critically and thoroughly examining ideas of all kinds, even those that are held dear.

Dialogue can occur both orally and in writing. In whole class and small group discussions, learners can engage in dialogue with each other about a variety of issues. Librarians and other educators should moderate the discussion by asking questions that will help learners better understand and explore their own perspectives. Richard W. Paul has advocated asking questions related to four main areas to help learners clarify their thinking about any issue:

1. origin (e.g., "How did you come to think this?")
2. support (e.g., "What is the evidence for this?")
3. conflicts with other perspectives (e.g., "How would you respond to the objection that . . . ?")
4. implications and consequences (e.g., "What are the consequences of believing this?")[5]

To promote dialogical thinking during discussions, librarians and other educators should also draw out the implications of certain comments, direct learners to proper sources and methods to use to help answer questions or clarify arguments, and emphasize that learners should only craft their responses after carefully listening to what others have said.

One type of instructional strategy that fosters good dialogue skills is the Socratic method. Based on Plato's writings, the *Socratic method* proceeds through a dialogue between a teacher and students about a philosophical or social question or some other issue that requires critical thinking. As the students discuss the issue, the teacher facilitates the discussion, asking questions that prompt learners to engage in thoughtful examination and consider alternative points of view. Learners draw upon their own experiences, and respond with ideas and questions of their own, as they listen carefully to others' ideas and acknowledge greater complexity in issues. Socratic questioning requires learners to explore different beliefs and think through their implications. In addition, the teacher models thoughtful listening, lets the dialogue develop organically, keeps learners focused on the original question or issue being discussed, and helps learners achieve a consensus about what they have learned through the dialogue.

Critical Thinking

In order to engage in productive dialogue that leads to learning, learners must use a variety of critical thinking skills. Critical thinking is an essential component of *information literacy*, which is the set of abilities associated with finding, retrieving, analyzing, and using information;[6] in fact, it is impossible to be information-literate without thinking critically.

Critical thinking can be defined in many ways. In some cases, scholars have used the term *critical thinking* to refer broadly to the use of higher-order thinking skills. Higher-order thinking skills include those that are represented at the higher levels of *Bloom's taxonomy*—a classification of the complexity of thinking skills—which include analysis, evaluation, and creation. These broad approaches to defining critical thinking state that it should be "purposeful, reasoned, and goal directed"[7] and should encompass thinking activities as diverse as problem-solving, creative thinking, decision-making, and scientific reasoning.

Other definitions have focused on the outcome of critical thinking, emphasizing that it involves the use of reason to decide "what to believe or do"[8] or that it concerns "weigh[ing] and evaluat[ing] information in a way that ultimately enables us to make informed decisions."[9] Finally, some scholars have defined critical thinking more narrowly as "judging the authenticity, worth, or accuracy of . . . a piece of information, a claim or assertion, or a source of data,"[10] or as "an active and systematic attempt to understand and evaluate arguments."[11]

Whether broad or narrow in scope, most definitions of critical thinking include a focus on the process of analyzing and evaluating information and the use of rigorous criteria in doing so.[12] Furthermore, in all of these definitions, the term *critical* implies that the thinker takes a questioning or analytical stance toward the information being evaluated. The discussion that proceeds below will focus on the narrower definition given above—that of analyzing and evaluating arguments.

An *argument* consists of a series of statements, including both *assertions* (claims that something is true) and *premises* (reasons or evidence that something is true), leading to a conclusion. Arguments may also contain *assumptions* (statements, often implied, for which there is no evidence). Sound arguments contain a clear and logical line of reasoning, as well as accurate premises that provide adequate support for the conclusion.

Analyzing arguments involves identifying their parts, including conclusions, premises, and *counterarguments*, or statements that refute the argument. In analyzing arguments, it is important to distinguish between *opinions* (assertions of a personal preference), *facts* (claims that are true), and *reasoned judgments* (preferences supported by sound arguments).[13]

Evaluating arguments involves making several judgment calls. Learners must evaluate the strength of the evidence used and whether certain evidence has been omitted. They must judge the credibility of the experts who made the statements in order to determine whether they can be trusted. They must also recognize faulty reasoning, often called *fallacies*. James R. Davis and Bridget D. Arend have provided several categories of common logical fallacies related to argumentation:

- fallacies regarding the structures of arguments (e.g., false dichotomies which suggest that only two choices are possible, overly simple explanations),
- fallacies regarding the incorporation of people into arguments (e.g., attacking a person instead of an argument, suggesting that a conclusion is valid because everyone supports it),
- fallacies regarding the use of language to make the arguments (e.g., stereotyping, use of emotional language),
- fallacies regarding the incorporation of evidence into arguments (biased information gathering, selective or irrelevant use of evidence),
- fallacies regarding other methods of providing support for arguments (e.g., appeals to authority or tradition), and
- fallacies regarding the conclusions drawn (e.g., overgeneralizing, jumping to or restating conclusions).[14]

Furthermore, some arguments are forms of *propaganda*, which are messages of suggestion conveyed through mass media that use powerful language and symbols to influence individual psychology.

While arguments may be presented in a variety of information sources, including written essays, online discussion postings, and verbal statements made by people engaged in discussion or debate, they may also consist of messages shared through imagery, advertising, social networks, or other forms of media. Librarians and other educators can help learners to analyze and evaluate the information found in all of these different types of information sources.

The practice of critical thinking helps to improve thinking and learning as learners become better able to identify and construct arguments that are clear, precise, and logical, and to become more aware of their own thinking processes and limitations. Critical thinking actually consists of a collection of different higher-order thinking skills and dispositions that help people approach situations or beliefs in a manner that facilitates learning. Discrete skills include analyzing parts of arguments, judging the credibility of sources, defining terms, detecting bias, identifying assumptions, recognizing logical inconsistencies, and determining the strength of arguments.[15] However, critical thinking skills can also be grouped into four larger, more encompassing areas:

1. *Knowledge in a discipline*, which enables learners to judge the value of evidence and come to better and faster conclusions
2. *Making inferences*, which refers to the process of making logical connections between pieces of information
3. *Evaluating information*, which includes analyzing, judging, and weighing evidence
4. *Metacognition*, which allows learners to reflect upon their own thinking processes, determine whether they are thinking in a manner that is fair or biased, and identify ways to improve[16]

Critical thinking dispositions include being open-minded and fair, being willing to examine one's own biases, and being committed to using credible sources and to expressing oneself with clarity and precision.[17]

The teaching of critical thinking skills centers around the notion that it is best to teach learners how to think rather than what to think. If learners are equipped with strong critical thinking skills, then they will be better positioned for lifelong learning. However, while information sources encountered in day-to-day life offer numerous opportunities to employ critical thinking skills, learners often neglect to use these skills for a variety of reasons. People are especially prone to refrain from thinking critically when reading sources found on the internet, perhaps because these sources appear to be authoritative or because they often appeal to emotions or use attention-grabbing strategies that prompt readers to engage without first taking a critical stance.

People can learn to employ critical thinking skills in everyday situations by becoming aware of common methods of persuasion and by applying this awareness to a variety of situations. Librarians and other educators can help learners use strategies to become aware of the ways that their own emotions affect their responses and interfere with critical thinking. They can also help learners to ask good questions about the messages they receive from legacy and social media, and they can help learners become more attuned to their own thinking patterns. Learners also need to become aware of the phenomenon of *confirmation bias*, which is the tendency to seek out and use information that supports or confirms their preexisting beliefs, and they should question whether their biases inhibit their ability to learn multiple approaches to understanding an issue.

Librarians and other educators can also help learners use the tools of critical thinking to clarify the reasons that underlie their own beliefs and preferences. They should help learners define their concepts with clarity, use language with precision, and consider the ways that concepts and categories relate to each other.[18] To enhance discussions, they can teach the skills of *argumentation*, a type of discourse in which learners take positions on issues, use evidence to support their ideas, and address opposing claims.

The Socratic method, discussed earlier, is an excellent pedagogical strategy for helping learners to strengthen their critical thinking skills by constructing sound arguments. When educators ask questions that challenge learners to clarify their thinking, specify their reasons and use of evidence, become aware of their inconsistencies, and probe their assumptions, they are helping learners to become more aware of their own thinking strategies and of the standards for high-quality thinking.[19]

IMPLICATIONS FOR LIBRARIES

A library can serve as a place where people from diverse backgrounds can come together to learn from each other through dialogue. Libraries can be forums for the practice of healthy community dialogues that promote the sharing of multiple perspectives, which in turn can enable people to arrive at deeper understandings of historical and contemporary issues.

Librarians can use some of the following strategies to integrate dialogical and critical thinking into library activities:

- Provide spaces that enable library patrons to assemble for debate and discussion. These might include spaces for small and large audiences and ones that contain features such as podiums and technology setups for audio and video projection.
- Circulate books, videos, and other resources that present multiple perspectives about a variety of historical and contemporary topics.
- Provide library collections and create collections of web resources that present pro-and-con arguments related to various contemporary issues.
- Expose learners to historical and contemporary primary sources and suggest strategies they can use when critically analyzing primary source information.
- Provide guidelines for evaluating text and image sources. Become community leaders in educating people about strategies they can use to critically evaluate information (e.g., related to politics, science, health care, etc.) obtained from online sources.
- Educate people about healthy and positive ways to discuss issues in social media forums.
- Hold training seminars and workshops for educators on strategies for teaching critical thinking as it relates to the use of information sources and information literacy.
- Host debates and panels about a variety of contemporary issues and invite speakers who represent diverse backgrounds to participate.
- Create a library-sponsored debate club.

TEACHING LIBRARIAN'S CORNER

When integrating dialogue into classes, librarians can focus discussions on issues related to disciplinary assignments and sources (e.g., history, literature, etc.) or on philosophical and values-related issues that are central to the use of information in contemporary society. To promote dialogical and critical thinking skills, librarians can ask questions, rephrase ideas, offer suggestions, and provide examples. They can also moderate discussions by responding, paraphrasing, summarizing, and clarifying to ensure that the conversation stays focused on the issues at hand and that all legitimate avenues are explored.

Librarians can use some of the following strategies to incorporate dialogical and critical thinking into instruction:

- Teach criteria for analyzing sources and arguments (e.g., strategies for identifying the credibility of a source such as the expertise of an author or corroboration with other sources) and detecting bias in sources (e.g., opinions presented as facts, appeals to emotion, overgeneralizations).
- Ask learners to practice identifying bias in primary and secondary sources by reading different sources on the same topic and identifying the perspective used in each one.
- Teach learners strategies for analyzing the messages presented in visual sources of information such as posters, ads, photographs, and info-graphics. Consider using sources that contain manipulation or misuse of an image and ask learners to analyze and discuss them.
- Incorporate panels and debates into in-class activities to help learners understand different points of view.
- Incorporate different forms of discussion into instruction sessions, including whole class discussion, small group discussion, and written responses in both in-person and online environments.
- Establish rules for respectful dialogue (e.g., listening respectfully with an open mind, not interrupting, addressing ideas rather than speakers) in order to create a safe discussion environment. Invite learners to reflect on what makes for good or bad discussions.
- Prepare questions in advance to begin discussions and keep them going if they start to peter out. Ask open-ended questions that prompt learners to more carefully evaluate evidence, clarify their reasoning, or analyze their assumptions. Avoid asking vague questions (e.g., "Any thoughts?") that confuse learners about how to respond.
- Center discussions around issues related to the use of information in society, such as: What information barriers exist that prevent people from making good decisions? Do the news media prioritize entertainment over truth? Is it possible to maintain privacy in the digital age? How can online communication be respectful? Who or what qualifies as an "authority"?
- When asking questions in whole class discussions, incorporate wait time by allowing for a few seconds of silence after asking questions in order to give learners time to think and respond. Stick with a line of questioning even if learners do not initially respond as you would like.

- Avoid relying too heavily on one or two learners to respond to all questions because others may learn that they do not need to participate. Consider that many learners are disinclined to participate in discussions for a variety of reasons (e.g., shyness, feeling unwelcome, fear of looking stupid, being a non-native language speaker). Advise these learners about effective ways to enter the conversation or encourage them to share their thoughts in other forums (e-mail, online discussions).

Using Questions to Prompt Critical Thinking

In *Discussion as a Way of Teaching*, Stephen D. Brookfield and Stephen Preskill described several types of questions that teachers can ask in the classroom to encourage deep engagement and critical thinking. Librarians can practice using these different types of questions in their own teaching:

- Questions that ask for more evidence (e.g., "Can you share information that supports your position?")
- Questions that ask for clarification (e.g., "Can you explain what you mean by that?")
- Open-ended questions that begin with words such as How? or Why? (e.g., "Why do you think that is?")
- Questions that link to or extend the ideas of other learners (e.g., "How does that relate to so-and-so's ideas?")
- Hypothetical questions that prompt learners to consider alternative outcomes (e.g., "What if the circumstances were changed in some way?")
- Cause-and-effect questions (e.g., "What effect might this situation have on a certain set of people?")[20]

FURTHER READING

Brookfield, Stephen D., and Stephen Preskill. *Discussion as a Way of Teaching: Tools and Techniques for Democratic Classrooms.* 2nd ed. San Francisco: Jossey-Bass, 2005.

Davis, James R., and Bridget D. Arend. *Facilitating Seven Ways of Learning: A Resource for More Purposeful, Effective, and Enjoyable College Teaching.* Sterling, VA: Stylus, 2012.

Saran, Rene, and Barbara Neisser. *Enquiring Minds: Socratic Dialogue in Education.* Stoke-on-Trent, UK: Trentham Books, 2004.

QUESTIONS TO CONSIDER

1. How does dialogical thinking enhance learning? What are some ways that libraries can bring people together to help them discuss and understand different points of view?

2. What are the challenges of using critical thinking to understand and analyze information sources found on the internet or through visual sources of information? What are some strategies that librarians can use to teach learners about these challenges?

3. Describe a discussion topic or question that could be used to engage a group of people (e.g., elementary students, college students, community members) in learning about the complexities of information exchange in the digital age.

NOTES

1. Nicholas C. Burbules, *Dialogue in Teaching: Theory and Practice* (New York: Teachers College Press, 1993), 8.

2. Burbules, *Dialogue in Teaching*, 121–22.

3. Richard Paul, *Critical Thinking: How to Prepare Students for a Rapidly Changing World* (Santa Rosa, CA: Foundation for Critical Thinking, 1995), 300; James R. Davis and Bridget D. Arend, *Facilitating Seven Ways of Learning: A Resource for More Purposeful, Effective, and Enjoyable College Teaching* (Sterling, VA: Stylus, 2012), 108–9.

4. Richard W. Paul, "Dialogical Thinking: Critical Thought Essential to the Acquisition of Rational Knowledge and Passions," in *Teaching Thinking Skills: Theory and Practice*, ed. Joan Boykoff Baron and Robert J. Sternberg (New York: Freeman, 1987), 127–48.

5. Paul, *Critical Thinking*, 297–98.

6. Association of College & Research Libraries, "Information Literacy Glossary," n.d., www.ala.org/acrl/issues/infolit/overview/glossary.

7. Diane F. Halpern, *Thought and Knowledge: An Introduction to Critical Thinking*, 3rd ed. (Mahwah, NJ: Lawrence Erlbaum Associates, 1996), 5.

8. Robert H. Ennis, "A Taxonomy of Critical Thinking Dispositions and Abilities," in *Teaching Thinking Skills: Theory and Practice*, ed. Joan Boykoff Baron and Robert J. Sternberg (New York: Freeman, 1987), 10.

9. Roger H. Bruning et al., *Cognitive Psychology and Instruction*, 4th ed. (Upper Saddle River, NJ: Pearson, 2004), 181.

10. Barry K. Beyer, *Practical Strategies for the Teaching of Thinking* (Boston: Allyn and Bacon, 1987), 33.

11. Richard Mayer and Fiona Goodchild, *The Critical Thinker*, 2nd ed. (Madison, WI: Brown & Benchmark, 1995), 2–3.

12. Paul, *Critical Thinking*, 21, 110.

13. Halpern, *Thought and Knowledge*, 201.

14. Davis and Arend, *Facilitating Seven Ways of Learning*, 118–20.

15. Beyer, *Practical Strategies for the Teaching of Thinking*, 27; Ennis, "A Taxonomy of Critical Thinking Dispositions and Abilities," 9–26.

16. Bruning et al., *Cognitive Psychology and Instruction*, 182–83.

17. Ennis, "A Taxonomy of Critical Thinking Dispositions and Abilities."

18. Davis and Arend, *Facilitating Seven Ways of Learning*, 117–18.

19. Paul, "Dialogical Thinking," 341–44.

20. Stephen D. Brookfield and Stephen Preskill, *Discussion as a Way of Teaching: Tools and Techniques for Democratic Classrooms*, 2nd ed. (San Francisco: Jossey-Bass, 2005), 87–91.

11

INQUIRY

THEORETICAL OVERVIEW

Asking questions can sometimes be just as important for learning as finding answers. And the process used to search for answers can sometimes be just as important as the final result of that search. This notion is captured by the idea of *inquiry*, a philosophical approach to teaching and learning that uses strategies related to asking and answering questions.

Librarians have played a central role in supporting inquiry-based learning on their campuses and in their communities, and inquiry is central to the practice of good information literacy skills. In fact, the Association of College and Research Libraries's information literacy framework notes the importance of the value of inquiry in its description of research as an "iterative" process that involves "asking increasingly complex or new questions whose answers in turn develop additional questions or lines of inquiry in any field."[1]

The role of inquiry in teaching and learning has a long history. One of the most prominent proponents of the importance of inquiry in education was John Dewey, whose educational philosophy is described below. In the modern classroom, inquiry approaches have been used across a variety of disciplines and levels, and their usage often varies depending on the subject matter, context, and needs of learners.

Inquiry and Knowledge Acquisition

John Dewey (1859–1952) was an American philosopher and educator who wrote many influential works in the late nineteenth and early twentieth centuries, including *Democracy and Education* (1916), *Logic: The Theory of Inquiry* (1938), and *Experience and Education* (1938). He advocated that educators encourage students to ask questions about issues of interest to them, think critically to solve problems, and develop a positive attitude toward learning.[2] Dewey was interested in the role of education in sustaining a democracy, which is strengthened when all citizens are prepared to capably participate to the fullest extent possible about issues that concern their lives. He described how the process of asking questions and finding solutions was part of being a good citizen. Dewey also described how schools help to transmit accumulated cultural knowledge so that learners are better prepared for communal participation. In addition, classrooms serve as smaller communities in which students can learn how to pursue inquiries within a social setting, benefit from the input of others, and understand how to make contributions that have broader relevance.[3]

Dewey believed that knowledge and understanding derive from experience. When learners have experiences, they interpret what happened using schemas, or mental frameworks, so that they are better prepared to deal with future experiences[4] (see chapter 1, "Constructing Knowledge"). Thus, thinking and doing are closely intertwined. Experience becomes a means through which learners understand the world around them.[5]

For Dewey, learning begins when a person encounters a problem that prevents them from acting in the normal way. Learners may become frustrated if they are unable to solve the problem using their current understanding. They then must search for solutions and experiment with different methods of solving the problem. When they find a solution that works, they learn new ways of responding to the problem and develop or alter their mental schemas for interpreting and organizing their experiences. This process of solving problems better prepares learners to deal with future experiences, adapt to new circumstances in a rapidly changing society, and gain greater control over their environment.[6]

Dewey described how people confront and learn from challenging problems through the process of inquiry. Inquiry begins when a person encounters a difficulty and progresses through the process of observing the problem in relation to some activity, exploring ideas and analyzing the problem, and using reasoning to generate and work through hypotheses. Inquiry then involves the testing of hypotheses, observing the consequences, and determining whether a reasonable solution has been discovered.[7] Dewey believed that the process of inquiry was the primary means through which learners acquire knowledge. In educational settings, the inquiry process is not only about solving the problem at hand but also about developing a positive orientation toward problem-solving that embraces curiosity, open-mindedness, and a love of learning, as a preparation for future life situations.

The process of inquiry has a communal component as well. In exploring possible responses to problems, learners should examine the ideas of others who have previously engaged in the inquiry process, and then incorporate that knowledge into their own understandings. Through its accumulation of shared knowledge, the community provides a resource for helping learners think through problems and develop hypotheses. In school settings, learners pursue inquiry within the social context of the classroom and can draw upon the knowledge of other students to help them generate ideas in response to difficult problems.

Dewey also recognized that the forming and revising of schemas is an emotional process. If learners become too emotionally attached to particular ideas, then they may be reluctant to engage in a process of inquiry that challenges their current way of thinking.[8] Because this process of mental revision is not only a difficult intellectual process but a challenging emotional process as well, it requires that learners take an active role in learning in order to ensure that change occurs.

Recognizing the importance of the mental, emotional, and experiential dimensions of learning, Dewey developed the notion of *child-centered education*, through which he advised that educators connect learning to learners' own interests and activities to increase their motivation to learn and connect their learning to the world of practical activity. When educators consider learners' experiences, they can make meaningful and relevant connections between traditional bodies of knowledge and children's lives.[9]

Inquiry-Based Instruction

Inquiry-based instruction is grounded in a constructivist approach to learning that focuses on the ways that learners construct their own mental models to help them make sense of the information they receive from the world around them. It therefore has connections to the work of Jean Piaget, who described the cognitive conflict that learners experience when confronting new information that conflicts with their existing mental schemas. Through the inquiry process, learners are forced to experience this imbalance in their mental structures and then revise them or develop new structures to explain this information (see chapter 1, "Constructing Knowledge").

An inquiry approach to teaching has the dual goals of increasing learner engagement and increasing knowledge and skills related to both disciplinary content and the inquiry process itself. Inquiry-based instruction values active learner engagement that begins with a learner's own interests and experiences. Inquiry learning projects have six main components:

1. Acquisition of new knowledge
2. Active pursuit of answers
3. Use of evidence to reach conclusions
4. Agency in the expression of one's own ideas
5. Complexity in the use of reasoning to find answers
6. Engagement with relevant communities[10]

Inquiry learning is often associated with discovery learning, which was first described by American educational psychologist Jerome S. Bruner (1915–2016) in the 1960s. *Discovery learning* describes how learners discover knowledge for themselves by investigating specific problems with minimal guidance and then use that information to generalize or abstract to larger concepts.[11] When teachers lecture to learners, thereby telling them the answers, they often deprive learners of the opportunity to generate and test their own ideas. When learners have the opportunity to ask questions about and investigate real-world situations, they are practicing the types of problem-solving skills that they will use throughout their lives. Learners are also better able to remember information for later use when they discover it for themselves.

An important emphasis of inquiry-based instruction is on the process of learning to think, rather than on knowing the "correct" answers. Thus, inquiry-based instruction helps to develop metacognitive awareness in learners—that is, awareness of one's own thinking processes (see chapter 6, "Self-Regulation"). Inquiry also helps learners to improve their critical thinking skills by learning to examine their own assumptions and beliefs, and distinguish between ideas and evidence (see chapter 10, "Dialogue"). Once learners can do this, they have better understanding and control of their own thought processes and are better prepared to apply the inquiry process to future situations.

Another important influence on current approaches to inquiry-based instruction comes from the work of Brazilian educator Paulo Freire (1921–1997). Freire called for a problem-posing approach to pedagogy whereby educators help learners reflect upon and ask questions about the problems experienced in their own lives in order to examine social conditions and possibilities for transformation.[12] Freire wanted learners to develop a *critical consciousness*, which involves an understanding that social conditions and knowledge structures are influenced by social and political forces that reinforce unequal power distributions. Once learners are able to recognize how these forces operate, they become empowered to work for change.[13] The influence of Freire and others advocating for critical pedagogy has resulted in methods that combine inquiry-based instruction with the development of critical consciousness and a focus on social action. Through *critical inquiry,* learners research issues related to power and privilege within social institutions. Learners take an analytical stance toward understanding power relationships and examine issues and questions that are relevant to their lives, often with the aim of developing action plans that attempt to change structures and systems that result in inequitable distributions of power.[14]

Various pedagogies have been developed that use an inquiry-based approach to learning. Here are a few examples that have been implemented across different grade levels and disciplines:

- *Place-based learning:* Learners study a particular place, including its artifacts, histories, peoples, structures, and ecologies. Learners investigate features of their immediate physical world, often take a critical stance toward their subjects, and engage in interdisciplinary research for authentic purposes and audiences.[15]
- *Problem-based learning:* Learners participate in guided exploration of complex, real-world problems. Learners are first given an ill-defined, often interdisciplinary, problem. Then, with the aid of a facilitator, they collaboratively identify and explore the problem and possible solutions, and often share what they have learned in the form of a final product or performance.[16]
- *Project-based learning:* Learners create meaningful artifacts within authentic contexts. Tasks begin with real-world questions that learners explore through questioning, problem-solving, and disciplinary research. Learners then collaborate to create projects that address the questions in ways that have meaning within a community context.[17]
- *Youth participatory action research:* Youth collaborate with adults in investigating real-world problems that concern their own lives. Drawing upon their own experience with local issues, learners collectively identify problems, conduct original research, and propose solutions. Their research is intended to lead to actions designed to raise awareness about social issues, while helping to develop a critical consciousness in learners.[18]

The Inquiry Process

The implementation of inquiry learning may vary across the disciplines, but it often follows a pattern which resembles that used in scientific exploration (see figure 11.1). The beginning of the process—question or idea identification—may be accomplished through initial exploration of or brainstorming about materials or phenomena. Often, educators may provide a general area of investigation, and then learners will develop specific questions and hypotheses about that area that can be explored through the use of evidence. Ideally, learners should explore issues that are meaningful and connect to their current knowledge, but their questions and hypotheses should also challenge their current ways of thinking. Learners should develop a plan for exploration that includes gathering evidence in any number of ways, such as the examination of secondary sources or the firsthand collection of data. Learners must then interpret the evidence and use analysis to find relationships and patterns in the data that allow them to answer their questions, or confirm or disprove their theories. Finally, through reflection, learners learn to apply

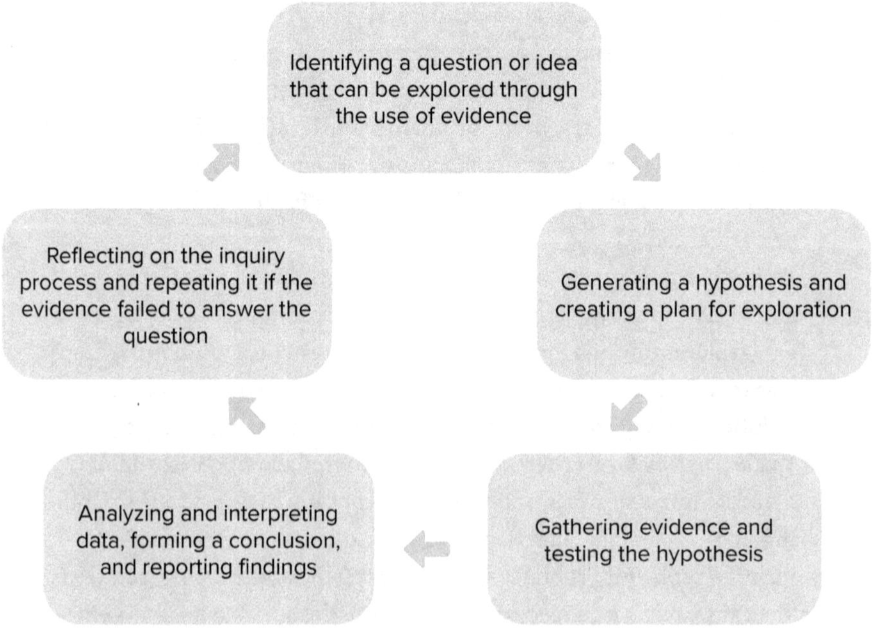

FIGURE 11.1

Stages in the process of learning through inquiry

their discoveries to new situations. They may also repeat the process if it failed to answer their question or use their discoveries to ask new questions that initiate the inquiry process again.

Although inquiry learning is often associated with science education, it is widely used across various subjects. In fact, a range of disciplinary content standards often refer to inquiry skills through language that describes identifying questions for investigation, forming hypotheses, or analyzing data. For instance, many of the Common Core's English Language Arts Standards, a set of national K–12 content standards used in the United States, require students to use evidence, analyze information, or investigate a topic in their writing.[19]

Librarians and other educators can play a critical role in helping to guide the inquiry process for learners. They often present problems or situations that require learners to use investigation skills. They serve as guides throughout the inquiry process by asking questions to help further learners' thinking, prompting them to consider problems from multiple perspectives, teaching disciplinary methods of investigation (e.g., conducting interviews, collecting data) and knowledge-sharing, and helping them to reflect upon what they learned. In addition, librarians and other educators can help to connect disciplinary content with learners' experiences and interests in order to generate engagement in the inquiry process.

Librarians and other educators must also gauge how much support learners need and adjust their instruction accordingly. This will vary depending on learners' ages, abilities, and levels of preparation. While university graduate students may be able to conduct investigations largely independently, learners at lower levels may need more guidance and structure. Indeed, in many cases, learners need considerable preparation and background information to be able to confidently investigate a problem. This may require that librarians and other educators use *direct instruction*, through which they directly present learners with the material to be learned, such as through lectures or demonstrations.

Librarians and other educators can provide different levels of support for learners pursuing a line of inquiry. In discussing inquiry for science education, Alan Colburn describes several teaching strategies that provide learners with different levels of support:

- *Structured inquiry:* The educator poses a problem to investigate, provides materials for investigation, and selects methods that learners will use, but learners conduct the analysis and draw their own conclusions.
- *Guided inquiry:* The educator poses a problem to investigate and provides materials for investigation, but learners devise their own methods for

analyzing the problem, in addition to conducting the analysis and drawing their own conclusions.

- *Open inquiry:* Learners develop their own questions for investigation, as
  well as obtaining materials, selecting the methods, analyzing the data,
  and drawing conclusions.[20]

With whatever method of inquiry is used, librarians and other educators should
pose questions throughout the process that guide learners to discover and construct knowledge.

Finally, librarians and other educators can also help to make connections
between learner inquiries and professional inquiries. While professional communities of inquiry, such as scientific communities, differ from classroom communities
in that the former are more interested in the creation of new knowledge or the
exploration of existing knowledge than in the process of learning, professional
inquiry processes may provide models for learners to follow. To teach these connections, librarians and other educators can introduce learners to some of the
processes used by professionals. At higher levels, learners may assist professionals
to solve problems in real-world contexts and then reflect upon their experiences in
classroom contexts.[21]

IMPLICATIONS FOR LIBRARIES

While inquiry-based learning has been used across the disciplines, inquiry
approaches can sometimes be challenging to implement in classroom and other
settings. Many educators have not been adequately prepared to teach inquiry, and
learners may not possess solid skills for investigation, even at the higher levels.
Many educators need assistance with teaching skills related to information-searching, research design, data collection, and data analysis. Learners often need considerable scaffolding support for inquiry endeavors, and they can benefit from
working with mentors who can help to guide them in the inquiry process. Because
inquiry-based learning projects can be resource-intensive, opportunities abound
for librarians to participate in these endeavors.

Librarians can use some of the following strategies to provide support for inquiry-based learning:

- Work with educators to purchase primary and secondary resources in
  a variety of formats and reading levels to support inquiry projects for
  learners of different ages and abilities. Textbooks usually do not provide
  adequate support for inquiry projects.

- Select primary sources that can be used as starting points for inquiry assignments. Promote primary sources, and create or provide materials that show learners how to use primary source collections.
- Provide equipment and resources that learners can check out to use for inquiry projects, such as robotics sets, building tools, and instruments such as microscopes.
- Provide and promote technologies that facilitate the inquiry process, such as software for quantitative and qualitative analysis.
- Partner with campus entities and programs (e.g., undergraduate research offices, honors programs, International Baccalaureate programs, science fairs) or community groups or initiatives (e.g., citizen science projects, www.citizenscience.gov) to develop inquiry-based tasks and provide support for learners engaged in those tasks.
- Hold book clubs or discussion groups to help learners reflect upon and ask questions about contemporary issues that can lead to further inquiry.
- Provide forums in the library for learners engaged in inquiry projects to connect with other learners, discuss their challenges, and provide support for each other.
- Sponsor professional development for educators about inquiry-based teaching strategies.
- Connect learners to professionals and mentors (through events and other activities) who can help model the inquiry process. Librarians can also serve as mentors themselves.
- Host science fairs, research symposiums, or other events where learners can present the results of their inquiry projects.

TEACHING LIBRARIAN'S CORNER

Librarians can use inquiry-based teaching strategies during both whole class instruction and one-on-one consultations. When working with individual learners, librarians should have thoughtful discussions with them about their inquiry topics. They should ask many questions that prompt learners to think critically about the process of idea formulation, information-searching, and research strategy development.

Librarians can use some of the following strategies to incorporate inquiry-based learning into their teaching:

- Collaborate with other educators to identify areas for investigation that are relevant and interesting to learners.
- Use structured question formulation strategies to help learners develop better research questions (e.g., the "question formulation technique" from the Right Question Institute, https://rightquestion.org).
- Teach strategies such as Ken Macrorie's "I-Search paper"[22] or related techniques that encourage learners to reflect upon and write narratives about their searches for answers to their questions.
- Model the process of moving from real-life experiences to research questions by talking through or role-playing examples.
- Use primary sources to help learners generate questions about events, pose theories, and challenge popular explanations.
- Use social annotation tools (e.g., Hypothesis, https://web.hypothes .is) to help learners collectively identify and understand key concepts from their readings that they can use to generate questions for further inquiry.
- Teach learners that trying out different topics and questions before settling on one to investigate is part of the research process. Promote experimentation and brainstorming. Encourage learners to discuss their research ideas with and offer feedback to each other.
- Teach disciplinary information sources to help learners grasp the language and communication styles used within the disciplines to structure inquiry. Include disciplinary visual information sources as appropriate, such as maps, diagrams, and charts.
- Emphasize the iterative nature of the question-asking process (i.e., finding answers leads to more questions) and the research process.

The I-Search Paper

The I-Search paper, a writing format developed by Ken Macrorie, demonstrates how reflective writing can be used to foster greater awareness about the process of asking questions and searching for answers. In the I-Search paper, learners tell the stories of their research processes in a way that is more personal and less formal than that found in a typical research paper. While the I-Search paper can be organized in different ways, Macrorie suggests four possible sections:

1. What I knew (and didn't know)
2. Why I'm writing this paper
3. The search
4. What I learned (or didn't learn)[23]

FURTHER READING

Duncan, Ravit Golan, and Clark Chinn, eds. *International Handbook of Inquiry and Learning.* New York: Routledge, 2021.

Kuhn, Deanna. *Education for Thinking.* Cambridge, MA: Harvard University Press, 2005.

Reale, Michelle. *Inquiry and Research: A Relational Approach in the Classroom.* Chicago: American Library Association, 2019.

QUESTIONS TO CONSIDER

1. Give an example of a primary source. How might a learner use that source to generate questions for an inquiry-based project? How might you design a lesson around that source?

2. What are some examples of projects that you could develop to connect inquiry-based learning to learners' own experiences during library instruction situations or library-hosted events?

3. What are some challenges that teachers and librarians might face when implementing inquiry-based learning projects? What are some ways that these challenges can be met?

NOTES

1. Association of College & Research Libraries, "Framework for Information Literacy for Higher Education," 2016, www.ala.org/acrl/standards/ilframework.

2. Richard Pring, *John Dewey: The Philosopher of Education for Our Time?* (London: Continuum, 2007), 6–7, 50–91; John Dewey, *Democracy and Education: An Introduction to the Philosophy of Education* (New York: Macmillan, 1916).

3. Dewey, *Democracy and Education.*

4. Pring, *John Dewey,* 62–65.

5. Dewey, *Democracy and Education,* 163–78.

6. Pring, *John Dewey,* 60–65.

7. Pring, *John Dewey,* 65–67; John Dewey, *Logic: The Theory of Inquiry* (New York: Henry Holt, 1938), 101–19.

8. Pring, *John Dewey,* 70.

9. Pring, *John Dewey,* 78–79, 90.

10. Clark A. Chinn and Ravit Golan Duncan, "Inquiry and Learning," in *International Handbook of Inquiry and Learning*, ed. Ravit Golan Duncan and Clark A. Chinn (New York: Routledge, 2021), 1–14.

11. Jerome S. Bruner, "The Act of Discovery," *Harvard Educational Review* 31 (1961): 21–32.

12. Paulo Freire, *Pedagogy of the Oppressed*, trans. Myra Bergman Ramos (New York: Bloomsbury Academic, 2000).

13. Freire, *Pedagogy of the Oppressed*; Paulo Freire, *Education for Critical Consciousness* (New York: Seabury, 1973).

14. Ben Kirshner, *Youth Activism in an Era of Education Inequality* (New York: NYU Press, 2015), 134–62; Karina Otoya-Knapp, "When Central City High School Students Speak: Doing Critical Inquiry for Democracy," *Urban Education* 39, no. 2 (2004): 149–71, https://doi.org/10.1177/0042085903260914.

15. Erin Donovan, "Learning to Embrace Our Stories: Using Place-Based Education Practices to Inspire Authentic Writing," *Middle School Journal* 47, no. 4 (2016): 23–31; David A. Gruenewald, "The Best of Both Worlds: A Critical Pedagogy of Place," *Educational Researcher* 32, no. 4 (May 2003): 3–12, https://doi.org/10.3102/0013189X032004003.

16. John R. Savery, "Overview of Problem-Based Learning: Definitions and Distinctions," *Interdisciplinary Journal of Problem-Based Learning* 1, no. 1 (2006): 9–20.

17. Emily C. Miller and Joseph S. Krajcik, "Promoting Deep Learning through Project-Based Learning: A Design Problem," *Disciplinary and Interdisciplinary Science Education Research* 1, no. 7 (2019): 1–10, https://doi.org/10.1186/s43031-019-0009-6.

18. Julio Cammarota and Michelle Fine, "Youth Participatory Action Research: A Pedagogy for Transformational Resistance," in *Revolutionizing Education: Youth Participatory Action Research in Motion*, ed. Julio Cammarota and Michelle Fine, *Critical Youth Studies* (New York: Routledge, 2008), 1–11.

19. Common Core State Standards Initiative, "English Language Arts Standards," 2022, https://learning.ccsso.org/common-core-state-standards-initiative.

20. Alan Colburn, "An Inquiry Primer," *Science Scope* 23, no. 6 (2000): 42–44.

21. S. R. Goldman et al., "Learning as Inquiry," in *International Encyclopedia of Education*, ed. Penelope Peterson, Eva Baker, and Barry McGaw, 3rd ed. (Oxford: Elsevier, 2010), 297–302, https://doi.org/10.1016/B978-0-08-044894-7.00495-4.

22. Ken Macrorie, *The I-Search Paper: Revised Edition of Searching Writing* (Portsmouth, NH: Heinemann, 1988).

23. Macrorie, *The I-Search Paper*, 64.

IMAGINATION

THEORETICAL OVERVIEW

Playing a game, building with blocks, designing a dress, drawing a sketch, solving a science problem. What do these activities have in common? All of them involve the imagination—that is, the formation of mental images or concepts. People's capacity to imagine not only improves their happiness and well-being, but it may also help them learn better.

Acts of imagination include both play and creative endeavors. While play may appear to be merely a pleasurable or even wasteful activity—one that is often opposed to the "productive" endeavor of work—it serves an important role in human development. Creative endeavors, ranging from the arts to the sciences and from large-scale creative acts to everyday forms of creative problem-solving, give purpose and meaning to human existence.

While libraries can be places for quiet contemplation and intense concentration, they are also places of fun, exploration, and imagination. Librarians can support imaginative learning by providing opportunities for play and creative expression.

Play

Although well-known for being enjoyable, play is somewhat difficult to define. *Play* is generally thought to define activities that are pleasurable, voluntary, and intrinsically motivated, that involve active engagement, and that often incorporate make-believe.[1]

In *Homo Ludens: A Study of the Play Element in Culture*, Dutch historian Johan Huizinga described play as

> a free activity standing quite consciously outside "ordinary" life as being "not serious", but at the same time absorbing the player intensely and utterly. It is an activity connected with no material interest, and no profit can be gained by it. It proceeds within its own proper boundaries of time and space according to fixed rules and in an orderly manner.[2]

Play may include activities such as constructing objects, rough-and-tumble physical engagement, role play, and rules-based sports and games, and it may or may not include the element of pretending.

Play is an essential part of childhood. Doris Pronin Fromberg and Doris Bergen characterized children's play as having the following characteristics:

- *Symbolic:* Children's play involves things, beings, or activities that are made to represent other things, beings, or activities.
- *Meaningful:* Children's imaginary play has a basis in meaningful, real-life experiences.
- *Pleasurable:* Children are pleasurably immersed during play.
- *Active, voluntary, and intrinsically motivated:* Children become fully and actively engaged during play in an activity they have selected.
- *Rule-governed:* Children's play is governed by rules, often unspoken, for how the play will unfold.
- *Episodic:* Children's play is not focused on outcomes or a logical narrative progression.[3]

While the nature of play changes as children age, play continues to be important in the lives of adults as well.

Various theories have attempted to understand the meaning and function of play. Some classical theories have described play as a way to release excess energy or to relax and recharge. Others have regarded play as a way for children to rehearse cultural roles and behaviors that they might later enact as adults, or to act out and release more primitive impulses.[4] Psychoanalytic theories of play, based in the work of Sigmund Freud, have viewed children's play as a means of working through difficult or stressful emotions and of understanding and achieving some sense of harmony with the external world.[5]

Cognitive theories of play that emerged in the twentieth century stressed the role of play as a critical element in children's development of higher-level thinking skills. For Jean Piaget, children's play provides opportunities to use their imaginations to interact with their environment and construct their understanding of the world through the processes of assimilating and accommodating new information[6] (see chapter 1, "Constructing Knowledge"). For Lev Vygotsky, children's imaginative play, which is free from realistic constraints, allows them to imbue objects (e.g., a stick) with the characteristics of other objects (e.g., a horse); this enables them to develop the ability to use symbolic thinking, which serves as the basis for language, abstract thought, and other higher-level cognitive skills.[7] Vygotsky also described how children's play becomes its own zone of proximal development, enabling children to use their imagination to experiment with new roles and new ideas in a safe environment, which helps them to grow beyond what they could do normally[8] (see chapter 13, "Guidance").

While people of all ages can learn through play, it is especially important for young children. When children learn through play, they are directing their own exploration and discovery, often with some guidance from an adult. Play provides children with a safe space in which to practice a variety of skills that support learning and cognitive growth. According to Otto Weininger and Susan Daniel, play involves

> creative patterns like changing, designing, questioning, combining, organizing, integrating, simplifying. It involves judgmental patterns for the child, like defining, choosing, contrasting, comparing, criticizing, and evaluating. It involves discriminating patterns such as collecting, re-organizing, classifying, matching, ordering, describing, explaining, communicating, identifying, and listening, and many others. As the child goes through these patterns in play, he learns to be attentive and to listen, to perceive and to understand, to try and to interpret and then to communicate.[9]

Play also contributes to the brain's ability to focus on academic tasks, enhances creativity and metacognitive awareness, and supports the learning of language, math, spatial, and problem-solving skills. The integration of play into educational contexts encourages children to develop positive attitudes toward learning and increases their self-efficacy and motivation.

Playful learning consists of both free play and guided play. With free play, a learner has full autonomy during play, but guided play combines a learner's freedom to explore with an educator's guidance.[10] Librarians and other educators can provide guidance in two main ways. First, they can provide the environment and materials that are connected to learning outcomes.[11] For example, a librarian might provide a collection of musical instruments for children to play on and explore, or a librarian might provide a variety of art supplies for children to use following storytime. Second, librarians and other educators can comment upon and ask questions during play in order to help learners focus on or make discoveries connected to learning outcomes.[12] For instance, a librarian might guide learners who are making an object in a makerspace by asking questions that prompt them to think about how they can use different tools. Guided play maintains a learner's agency in play while integrating the educator's guidance and feedback that help them learn.

Different types of play—including physical play, constructive play, sociodramatic play, and games with rules— support the learning of different types of skills, as shown in table 12.1. In addition to engaging in different types of play, the nature of play changes as children age. In the early years, children more commonly play with objects and engage in imaginary play; as they grow older, they may increasingly play games with rules. Over time, the games they play, such as board games and games of sport, are likely to require more players and to demonstrate greater complexity in terms of roles, rules, and other features.

Creativity

Like play, creativity involves the human capacity to imagine, but with creative acts, the final product or result is important. Creativity concerns the use of the imagination to generate novel ideas or outcomes.[13] Creativity is important both for realizing personal satisfaction and for achieving growth in a knowledge economy. Indeed, modern progress depends on the creation of new products and solutions in response to complex problems, and jobs often require people to imagine possibilities, embrace new ideas, think of original solutions, and be flexible and open to change.

Historical views of creativity have centered around notions of genius, divine inspiration, and extraordinary examples of artistic expression, but modern conceptions have also focused on more commonplace creative acts that result from the combined influence of cognitive skills, motivation, personality, and environment. In the literature on creativity, a distinction is often made between "big C" creativity, which describes unusual achievements that are highly influential and transformative, and "little c" creativity, which describes everyday acts of dealing with problems in imaginative and flexible ways.[14] While few people may achieve acts of "big C" creativity, everyone is capable of being creative on a smaller scale, and indeed, people can learn strategies for becoming more creative in their lives and work.

TABLE 12.1

Learning and types of play

TYPE OF PLAY	CHARACTERISTICS	HOW IT SUPPORTS LEARNING
Physical play	Involves the use of movement and often takes place out of doors; may include "rough-and-tumble" activities.	Players develop motor coordination and learn the value of practice and focus in improving their movement skills.[15] They also improve their social skills when interacting with others.
Constructive play	Involves the use of objects to make something, such as drawing, building with blocks, or assembling items using computer software.	Players plan, follow sequences and models, create patterns, solve problems, and reflect upon what works.[16]
Sociodramatic play	Involves pretend play in which two or more players assume roles based on real-world situations, communicating with each other about how the play situation will unfold.	Players imagine the thoughts, feelings, and motives of other people, recognize their own similarities and differences, and come to a greater awareness of themselves. They also internalize cultural expectations and social rules by pretending to play roles learned from their culture. They improve their problem-solving skills as they think through different situations and improve their language skills by experimenting with different voices, narrative strategies, and vocabularies.[17]
Games with rules	Involves competitive play consisting of prescribed activities within situations bounded by rules that culminate in a particular outcome. Games may be physical (e.g., hide and seek) or mental (e.g., chess) in orientation.	Players use logic and reasoning, make decisions, think through problems, apply spatial and mathematical skills, create mental maps, and think abstractly. They also practice regulating their own behavior according to the rules of play, focus and sustain their attention, react quickly, and cooperate and negotiate with others.[18]

A creative idea, approach, or product has three main characteristics:

1. *Novel:* Newness or originality may be understood in a variety of contexts, including ideas that are new to the creator, new for an audience who receives them, or new for the discipline as a whole.
2. *Effective:* Creative products should succeed in achieving their goals. In other words, they should be pleasing, useful, or solve a problem.
3. *Ethical:* Creative acts should achieve a purpose that is moral, helpful, or honorable. Acts that are harmful or unethical, even if those acts are novel and effective, are not usually considered to be creative.[19]

The term *creative learning* describes learning that enhances creativity. Through creative learning, learners can be imaginative, generate ideas, pose different or unusual solutions, ask questions, challenge the conventional, take ownership of their own learning, and express themselves in different ways.[20] Giving learners the freedom to be imaginative not only enhances their creativity, but also leads to improvements in learning of all kinds. In fact, the processes of creativity and learning are closely related as is demonstrated by constructivist learning theory, which describes how learners construct new knowledge and create their own understandings of the world[21] (see chapter 1, "Constructing Knowledge").

The practice of being creative involves numerous cognitive processes that are also beneficial for learning. First, creativity involves divergent thinking, which is the production of many, varied, and possibly original responses to a situation or problem. Divergent thinking is often opposed to convergent thinking, which uses logic to arrive at a single, best solution to a problem.[22] Other skills include conceptual combination, which refers to combining different ideas in new ways, and conceptual expansion, which involves modifying existing concepts to include new ideas.[23] The generation of metaphors, analogies, mental models, and images is useful in enabling learners to make links among concepts in order to lead to new insights.[24] Creative thinking also involves synthesizing information, combining new and old information, evaluating combinations of information, forming associations, transforming information into different elements, seeing issues from different perspectives, merging ideas from different disciplines, and constructing abstractions based on concrete information.[25]

Traditional views of the creative process have held that creativity is enacted through four major steps: preparation, incubation, illumination, and verification (see figure 12.1). This view holds that, after thinking about a problem and gathering information about it, creators experience a period of often unconscious reflection,

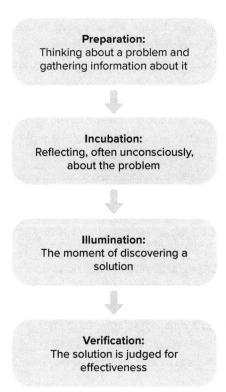

Preparation:
Thinking about a problem and gathering information about it

Incubation:
Reflecting, often unconsciously, about the problem

Illumination:
The moment of discovering a solution

Verification:
The solution is judged for effectiveness

FIGURE 12.1

Steps in the traditional view of the creative process

followed by an "ah ha!" moment of discovery and a judgment about whether the discovered solution is effective.[26]

Other descriptions of the creative process have focused on the role of *problem-solving*, which involves coming up with solutions for situations that lack clear answers.[27] Problems that are ill-defined—meaning that they lack clear goals, complete information, or explicit methods of solving—are especially likely to require creative or divergent thinking skills in order to arrive at solutions.[28] Creative problem-solving combines both divergent and convergent thinking skills to arrive at solutions to ill-defined problems. The creative problem-solving process involves identifying problems, finding and examining data, setting goals for problem-solving, exploring a variety of possible solutions, evaluating possibilities, and devising a solution.[29]

Gaining fluency or expertise within a particular discipline supports the development of creative thinking skills. The novelty that characterizes creative thinking is derived from combining existing ideas in new ways. This means that in addition to possessing certain types of cognitive skills, a creative learner must also have a solid base of knowledge and skills within a particular field, so that they have a broad range of disciplinary information with which to explore new possibilities.[30] Moreover, for acts of creativity to be recognized, they have to be communicated in such a way that people can recognize and understand them, which often means that the creator must effectively communicate in the language or methods of the discipline.[31]

Librarians and other educators can promote creative thinking skills in numerous ways. They should establish a supportive social environment to give learners a safe space in which learners can try new things. They can foster learners' intrinsic motivation and encourage learners to pursue areas of interest, even if those areas are fanciful or unusual. Finally, librarians and other educators can integrate music, theater, or other creative arts into lessons and activities. The practice of the creative arts can be especially beneficial in helping learners to better understand the human experience and to develop complex thought processes, including the ability to recognize patterns, create mental representations, think symbolically or metaphorically, and observe and respond to details.[32] As opposed to more traditional approaches, the use of imaginative activities often entices learners to respond with greater engagement, flexibility, and openness, which in turn helps to develop learner creativity.

IMPLICATIONS FOR LIBRARIES

Librarians can provide the environments, materials, and tools that encourage and support creative thinking and play. When facilitating creative activities, librarians should be open to and supportive of the expression of different and unusual ideas, and encourage learners to show respect for and avoid criticizing the ideas of their peers. When facilitating play, librarians can provide periods of free play followed by more directed learning activities. For instance, librarians might introduce materials and allow learners to explore with them before moving to a more guided play situation in which they ask questions and provide suggestions focused on a learning outcome. However, if they intervene too much, they may undermine the playfulness of the situation and change it from being a learner-driven activity.

Librarians can use some of the following strategies to integrate the imagination into library activities:

- Provide spaces for play and games and fill them with playful objects and materials. Create spaces such as flower gardens, musical instrument collections, and mazes, as well as spaces that allow for building things, working with robotics, manipulating large-scale maps, and so on.

- Provide makerspaces, media labs, and virtual reality studios that allow learners to tinker, design, experiment, and play. Host workshops or camps in these spaces that teach artistic, writing, media, or coding skills and teach learners how to make creative products (e.g., making books).
- Use physical games to help learners understand their library, community, and contemporary issues (e.g., scavenger and treasure hunts, geocaching, escape rooms).
- Provide access to video games or digital experiences that support learning (e.g., virtual field trips that allow learners to use the internet to "visit" and learn about various places).
- Host game nights or family game days. Provide games and puzzles for checkout.
- Host design challenges that encourage learners to use their creative skills to make projects.
- Celebrate holidays or days of local significance with arts and crafts activities and performances.
- Invite speakers and artists who model creative processes, have solved unique problems, or can stimulate learners' curiosity about a variety of topics. Host performances that represent a variety of areas (e.g., music, dance, magic) featuring performers from a variety of backgrounds.
- Engage with learners who are involved in play by commenting upon and asking questions about their play explorations. Moderate dramatic play to direct learners' energies in positive ways and avoid conflicts.
- Follow storytimes and events with opportunities for learners to respond by using their imaginations. For example, learners can respond through the visual arts (e.g., drawing, painting), creative writing (e.g., poems, stories), movement, or drama. Have play kits on hand that include various materials for making things (Legos, Play-Doh, paper, paint, hats, popsicle sticks, tape, blocks, markers), and integrate these kits into events and activities.
- Exhibit creative products made by learners, community members, artists, scientists, and others.

TEACHING LIBRARIAN'S CORNER

Teaching librarians can foster the imagination by encouraging learners to try new things and experiment with new approaches and by integrating games and the creative arts into learning situations. Librarians can also teach divergent thinking strategies, which are designed to increase the fluency (i.e., quantity), flexibility (i.e., diversity), and originality (i.e., uniqueness) of ideas.[33] Common strategies include techniques such as mind-mapping and brainstorming. With *mind-mapping*, learners create a visual representation of a theme (usually featured in the center of a diagram), with other shapes representing a diverse range of related ideas and lines representing associations between those ideas. With *brainstorming*, learners identify a problem and then generate as many ideas as possible to address the problem without censoring themselves. They should be as fanciful as they like and should practice combining and elaborating on ideas to generate new ideas. Once the process of idea generation has ended, learners should decide upon the criteria for judging their ideas and then select the best solution.

Librarians can use some of the following strategies to incorporate creativity and play into their teaching:

- Give learners choices about how they express their learning. For instance, instead of expressing their ideas in written form, can learners draw a picture or create a diagram instead? Set clear goals and expectations for learning but give learners freedom in how they achieve these goals.
- Encourage learners to ask questions, identify problems, pose original ideas, and discuss their thought processes. Be open to learners' ideas and encourage approaches that are unusual, different, or unexpected. Avoid being overly judgmental.
- Integrate social or community problems into instruction and invite learners to be creative in thinking about solutions.
- Ask open-ended questions that encourage learners to be imaginative, generate ideas, or see things from different points of view: questions such as "What parts or elements of this could be changed? How could this concept be modified? How could concepts be combined to create something new?"[34]
- Incorporate opportunities for individual and group brainstorming, mind-mapping, creating images and visualizations, creating models, and developing metaphors and analogies. For instance, when researching a topic, can learners create an analogy to help explain a process? Can they create a mind map of their project's structure?
- Use variations of brainstorming, such as reverse brainstorming, in which learners generate ideas that are the opposite of those desired; and pass-the-idea, in which learners write ideas on a piece of paper and pass

it to another learner who can change the idea or add a new idea before passing it on again.[35] These can be useful ways to explore project designs in a makerspace or generate ideas for a community research project.

- Teach design thinking strategies for makerspace projects. *Design thinking* involves inspiration (exploring and brainstorming problems and solutions), ideation (developing and testing ideas), and implementation (bringing solutions to fruition) in a process that includes understanding problems from the user's point of view and creating and testing prototypes.[36]

- Bring in readings from primary sources, and prompt learners to use them as the basis for asking questions, role-playing, or creative writing. What kinds of questions do the sources prompt? What kinds of problems emerge? Ask learners to explore the sources by using "who, what, where, when, why, and how" question prompts.

- Ask learners to role-play scenarios related to information literacy or to issues being researched (e.g., putting the truthfulness of information claims on trial). Use role play to help learners understand issues from different points of view.

Games in Library Instruction

For many years librarians have used games to teach library, research, information literacy, and other skills to learners of all ages. The use of games supports learning in various ways. They capture learners' attention by adding novelty and unpredictability, and they increase motivation by adding an element of fun and challenge. They involve learners in a hands-on activity, which can aid in constructing knowledge while providing scaffolded situations to support learners in the acquisition of new skills. Video games incorporate multimedia elements for learning, while physical or board games often require learners to collaborate with each other.

Some examples of common games used in library instruction include quiz shows such as *Jeopardy*, crossword puzzles, word games, and trivia games. Many games are structured as quests in which players must find something in a process that resembles information-searching. Physical quests, such as scavenger hunts, geocaching (which employs GPS for finding objects), and mysteries, require learners to go to different locations on their campus or in their community. Video quests may require learners to solve a mystery or find a treasure online in the context of an imaginative scenario.[37]

To be effective tools for learning, games should have clear, uncomplicated rules for playing so that learners can focus on the game itself without getting bogged down in its parameters.

FURTHER READING

Cropley, Arthur J. *Creativity in Education and Learning: A Guide for Teachers and Educators*. London: Kogan Page, 2001.

Fromberg, Doris Pronin, and Doris Bergen. *Play from Birth to Twelve: Contexts, Perspectives, and Meanings*. 2nd ed. New York: Routledge, 2006.

Starko, Alane J. *Creativity in the Classroom: Schools of Curious Delight*. 2nd ed. Mahwah, NJ: Lawrence Erlbaum Associates, 2001.

QUESTIONS TO CONSIDER

1. Pick an age level for a group of learners. List the different types of play described in this chapter and provide examples of how libraries can support learning for those learners through each of these types of play.

2. Think of a problem facing a library of your choice. Brainstorm possible solutions to the problem. Generate as many ideas—even if they are silly or fanciful—as possible without censoring yourself. Take a break and examine your list. Do any of the ideas seem feasible? If not, what would make them so?

3. Design an event or activity for a library of your choice that engages users in creative thinking and learning.

NOTES

1. Kathy Hirsh-Pasek, Roberta Golinkoff, and Diane Eyer, *Einstein Never Used Flash Cards: How Our Children Really Learn—and Why They Need to Play More and Memorize Less* (Emmaus, PA: Rodale, 2004), 210–11; Catherine Garvey, Play (Cambridge, MA: Harvard University Press, 1990), 4–5.

2. Johan Huizinga, *Homo Ludens: A Study of the Play-Element in Culture* (New York: Roy, 1950), 13.

3. Doris Pronin Fromberg and Doris Bergen, "Introduction," in *Play from Birth to Twelve: Contexts, Perspectives, and Meanings*, ed. Doris Pronin Fromberg and Doris Bergen, 2nd ed. (New York: Routledge, 2006), xviii.

4. Michael J. Ellis, *Why People Play* (Englewood Cliffs, NJ: Prentice Hall, 1973), 23–48; Olivia N. Saracho, "Theoretical Framework of Developmental Theories of Play," in *The Sage Handbook of Outdoor Play and Learning*, ed. Tim Waller et al. (London: Sage, 2017), 25–39, https://doi.org/10.4135/9781526402028.

5. Ellis, *Why People Play*, 64–70; Saracho, "Theoretical Framework of Developmental Theories of Play."

6. Ellis, *Why People Play*, 64–70; Jean Piaget, *Play, Dreams and Imitation in Childhood* (New York: W. W. Norton, 1962).

7. L. S. Vygotsky, "Play and Its Role in the Mental Development of the Child," *International Research in Early Childhood Education* 7, no. 2 (2016): 3–25.

8. L. S. Vygotsky, *Mind in Society: The Development of Higher Psychological Processes*, ed. Michael Cole (Cambridge, MA: Harvard University Press, 1978), 102.

9. Otto Weininger and Susan Daniel, *Playing to Learn: The Young Child, the Teacher and the Classroom* (Springfield, IL: Thomas, 1992), 29–30.

10. Kelly Fisher et al., "Playing Around in School: Implications for Learning and Educational Policy," in *The Oxford Handbook of the Development of Play*, ed. Anthony D. Pellegrini (New York: Oxford University Press, 2011), 342–60, https://doi.org/10.1093/oxfordhb/9780195393002.001.0001.

11. Deena Skolnick Weisberg et al., "Guided Play: Principles and Practices," *Current Directions in Psychological Science* 25, no. 3 (2016): 177–82, https://doi.org/10.1177/0963721416645512.

12. Weisberg et al., "Guided Play."

13. Anna Craft, *Creativity in Schools: Tensions and Dilemmas* (Abingdon, UK: Routledge, 2005), 20, 53, https://doi.org/10.4324/97802033579614.

14. Craft, *Creativity in Schools*, 19; Arthur J. Cropley, *Creativity in Education and Learning: A Guide for Teachers and Educators* (London: Kogan Page, 2001), 10–11; Beth A. Hennessey and Teresa M. Amabile, "Creativity," *Annual Review of Psychology* 61 (2010): 569–98.

15. Doris Bergen, "Reconciling Play and Assessment Standards: How to Leave No Child Behind," in *Play from Birth to Twelve: Contexts, Perspectives, and Meanings*, ed. Doris Pronin Fromberg and Doris Bergen, 2nd ed. (New York: Routledge, 2006), 233–416.

16. George Forman, "Constructive Play," in *Play from Birth to Twelve: Contexts, Perspectives, and Meanings*, ed. Doris Pronin Fromberg and Doris Bergen, 2nd ed. (New York: Routledge, 2006), 103–117.

17. Doris Pronin Fromberg, *Play and Meaning in Early Childhood Education* (Boston: Allyn and Bacon, 2002), 21–27; Doris Pronin Fromberg, "Play's Pathways to Meaning: A Dynamic Theory of Play," in *Play from Birth to Twelve: Contexts, Perspectives, and Meanings*, ed. Doris Pronin Fromberg and Doris Bergen, 2nd ed. (New York: Routledge, 2006), 159–18.

18. Constance Kamii and Yasuhiko Kato, "Play and Mathematics at Ages One to Ten," in *Play from Birth to Twelve: Contexts, Perspectives, and Meanings*, ed. Doris Pronin Fromberg and Doris Bergen, 2nd ed. (New York: Routledge, 2006), 187–98; Ed Baines and Peter Blatchford, "Children's Games and Playground Activities in School and Their Role in Development," in *The Oxford Handbook of the Development of Play*,

ed. Anthony D. Pellegrini (New York: Oxford University Press, 2011), 260–83, https://doi.org/10.1093/oxfordhb/9780195393002.001.00013.

19. Cropley, *Creativity in Education and Learning*, 6–15.

20. Craft, *Creativity in Schools*, 54–61; Pat Thomson and Julian Sefton-Green, *Researching Creative Learning: Methods and Issues* (London: Taylor & Francis Group, 2010), 2.

21. Craft, *Creativity in Schools*, 53; Cropley, *Creativity in Education and Learning*, 28.

22. Hennessey and Amabile, "Creativity"; Richard E. Mayer, "Problem Solving," in *Encyclopedia of Creativity*, ed. Mark A. Runco and Steven R. Pritzker, vol. 2, 2 vols. (San Diego, CA: Academic, 1999), 437–47.

23. Thomas B. Ward, Steven M. Smith, and Jyotsna Vaid, "Conceptual Structures and Processes in Creative Thought," in *Creative Thought: An Investigation of Conceptual Structures and Processes,* ed. Thomas B. Ward, Steven M. Smith, and Jyotsna Vaid (Washington, DC: American Psychological Association, 1997), 1–27.

24. Ward, Smith, and Vaid, "Conceptual Structures and Processes in Creative Thought."

25. Cropley, *Creativity in Education and Learning*, 31–35.

26. Alane J. Starko, *Creativity in the Classroom: Schools of Curious Delight*, 2nd ed. (Mahwah, NJ: Lawrence Erlbaum Associates, 2001), 25–27; Graham Wallas, *The Art of Thought* (New York: Harcourt, Brace, 1926), 79–107.

27. Mayer, "Problem Solving."

28. Mayer, "Problem Solving"; Richard E. Ripple, "Teaching Creativity," in *Encyclopedia of Creativity*, ed. Mark A. Runco and Steven R. Pritzker, vol. 2, 2 vols. (San Diego, CA: Academic, 1999), 629–38.

29. Starko, *Creativity in the Classroom*, 27–32; Alex F. Osborn, *Applied Imagination: Principles and Procedures of Creative Thinking*, revised ed. (New York: Scribner, 1957).

30. Craft, *Creativity in Schools*, 28; Cropley, *Creativity in Education and Learning*, 45; Arthur J. Cropley, "Education," in *Encyclopedia of Creativity*, ed. Mark A. Runco and Steven R. Pritzker, vol. 1, 2 vols. (San Diego, CA: Academic, 1999), 629–42.

31. Cropley, *Creativity in Education and Learning*, 16.

32. David A. Sousa, *How the Brain Learns*, 5th ed. (Thousand Oaks, CA: Corwin, 2016), 214-217.

33. Ripple, "Teaching Creativity."

34. Starko, *Creativity in the Classroom*, 174–80.

35. Starko, *Creativity in the Classroom*, 168–74.

36. Tim Brown, "Design Thinking," *Harvard Business Review* 86, no. 6 (2008): 84–141.

37. Maura A. Smale, "Learning through Quests and Contests: Games in Information Literacy Instruction," *Journal of Library Innovation* 2, no. 2 (2011): 36–55; Megan Margino, "Revitalizing Traditional Information Literacy Instruction: Exploring Games in Academic Libraries," *Public Services Quarterly* 9, no. 4 (October 2013): 333–41, https://doi.org/10.1080/15228959.2013.842417.

GUIDANCE

THEORETICAL OVERVIEW

How much guidance do learners need? What forms should it take? And how is this best determined? These are questions that every educator considers when working with learners.

The notion of the *zone of proximal development* addresses how the learning process occurs through collaboration with and guidance from a teacher who tailors the learning experience to the learner's potential for development.[1] Because librarians often assist learners in a variety of situations, the zone of proximal development provides a useful framework upon which to consider how this guidance is enacted.

The zone of proximal development has influenced many ways that educators approach instruction in one-on-one, small group, and whole class contexts, and has been influential in the development of several instructional practices, such as scaffolding and guided participation, which are reviewed below.

The Zone of Proximal Development

The zone of proximal development was first described by Lev Vygotsky,[2] who was interested in the ways that social context influences the development of higher-level psychological functions such as concept formation, voluntary attention, and logical memory. He was influential in contributing to the sociocultural theory of development (described in chapter 2, "Collaboration"), which describes how individuals' cognitive development relates to cultural, historical, and institutional contexts.

As part of this theory, Vygotsky conceptualized thinking as an inherently collaborative or shared process. He showed that cognitive development originates in the social world before being internalized for individual psychological functioning. Not only does an individual's culture shape what that person learns, but the social interactions that occur within a culture influence how learning occurs. The zone of proximal development explains the "how" of learning by focusing on the role of interpersonal connections.

Vygotsky described the zone of proximal development as

> the distance between the actual development level as determined by independent problem-solving and the level of potential development as determined through problem-solving under adult guidance or in collaboration with more capable peers. . . . The zone of proximal development defines those functions that have not yet matured but are in the process of maturation, functions that will mature tomorrow but are currently in an embryonic state.[3]

In other words, a child's learning potential consists of the emerging cognitive tasks that they can perform with assistance from an adult or more knowledgeable member of the culture who explains and models concepts for the child, thus guiding their learning (see figure 13.1). In this sense, providing instructional guidance is not merely about addressing what a learner is currently capable of doing, but about focusing on a learner's potential.

The zone of proximal development simultaneously addresses two factors: the assessment of a learner's capabilities and the instructional practices that should be used to guide learning.[4] It is established through the dynamic interaction that occurs between the adult/teacher and child/learner. Once an adult recognizes the higher-level functions that are emerging in a child and determines the potential for growth, the child learns to execute tasks—first with assistance and then independently through practice. An adult engages the child in learning activities, models learning strategies, and guides the child to arrive at a new level of understanding. Through these interactions, the child also comes to understand how the adult approaches issues in a way that reflects the values and activities of the community, thereby perpetuating cultural practices and linking learning to cultural perspectives.

Vygotsky described how collaboration is at the heart of the zone of proximal development, for "in collaboration the child can always do more than he can independently."[5] Not only does the communication that occurs between the teacher and learner make possible greater growth than could be achieved alone, but the learner is an active participant in the dialogue. The learner contributes their own abilities

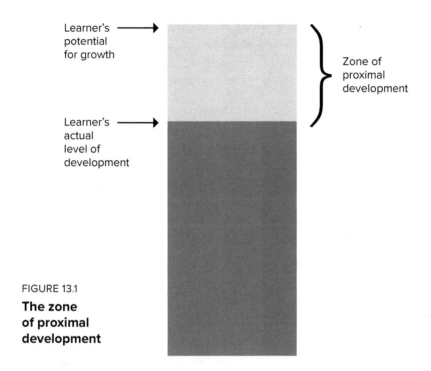

FIGURE 13.1

**The zone
of proximal
development**

and interests to the learning interaction, and the teacher actively responds to the learner's needs in a genuinely collaborative process, potentially learning as well. Thus, the zone of proximal development supports the notion that collaboration and dialogue are fundamental to the learning process.

Scaffolding and Guided Participation

Scaffolding is an instructional practice that has its basis in the zone of proximal development. The metaphor of a scaffold suggests the structural support system used during building construction. With *scaffolding*, a teacher or other expert assesses the support that a learner needs to complete a task and provides just enough assistance to enable a learner to complete it successfully. David Wood, Jerome S. Bruner, and Gail Ross originally described scaffolding as assistance that

> enables a child or novice to solve a problem, carry out a task, or achieve a goal which would be beyond his unassisted efforts. This scaffolding consists essentially of the adult "controlling" those elements of the task that are initially beyond the learner's capacity, thus permitting him to concentrate upon only those elements that are within his range of competence.[6]

Just like the temporary scaffolding used in building construction, the teacher's support is gradually removed as the learner acquires more proficiency, and eventually the learner is able to complete the task without assistance.

Effective scaffolding can be characterized by the following:

- *Shared goals:* The learner and teacher have a shared sense of purpose and ownership of the activity.
- *Appropriateness:* The instruction builds on the learner's current knowledge and skills.
- *Structure:* The teacher makes the structure of the learning clear, and the instruction embodies a natural sequence of thought and activity.
- *Dialogue and interaction:* The learner participates actively, and the teacher listens and responds to the learner's input.
- *Adaptive support:* The teacher adapts the support on the basis of the learner's progress.
- *Internalization:* The learner internalizes what has been learned, and control of the task shifts to the learner.[7]

Support can be provided not just on a cognitive level, but on an affective level as well, as the teacher helps a learner to manage the frustration they may experience during challenging tasks.

Guided participation is another instructional method that has a basis in the zone of proximal development. *Guided participation* refers to a learner's acquisition of knowledge and skills by participating in socially meaningful activities under the guidance of someone with greater experience.[8] It was first described by American psychologist Barbara Rogoff, who based this concept on the customs surrounding apprenticeship that are characteristic of various societies.[9]

Through guided participation, learners participate in authentic tasks that have communal value in collaboration with more skillful members of that community. For instance, a young child might learn about baking by helping a parent make a birthday cake. In this example, the parent measures out the ingredients and the child adds them to a bowl. The parent then gives the child a spoon and shows the child how to mix the batter. They work together to decorate the top of the cake in a way that is appropriate for their celebration.

With guided participation, people learn new skills or abilities by actively participating in culturally meaningful activities alongside a more experienced person who selects and structures the activities and provides explicit or indirect guidance.[10] Under guided participation, people learn within the zone of proximal development as determined by an expert who assists and collaborates with the learner. The expert offers explicit guidance in the form of direct instruction, modeling (described in chapter 5, "Observation"), or scaffolding, and implicit guidance through the arrangement of the activity and the environment in which it occurs. With guided participation, the learning context is critical, and the learner interacts with the environment in a dynamic fashion. Guided participation may also assist learners who have recently joined a community of practice to move from peripheral to full participation (described in chapter 9, "Context").

Guided participation can occur in a variety of settings, including work and home, and is common in natural learning and occupational learning contexts. While examples of learning through guided participation are common in everyday situations, such as the cake example cited above, it can also be used in a class or workshop. For instance, librarians and other educators can use guided participation by selecting a culturally valued task, structuring the learners' participation in the activity, and participating alongside them in the execution of that activity. Guided participation also frequently occurs during library mentoring and internship situations. For example, a library intern might work with a librarian to create an online library guide for a class or subject area. The librarian might instruct the intern in how to use the software to make the guide, point her to some examples of resources to include, and encourage her to apply her past experiences with online learning to the task. Together, they collaborate to produce the guide, with each person fully participating in its creation.

....

Peer Research Consultants and Scaffolding

While librarians can provide scaffolding support for learners, peers can also provide scaffolding during peer tutoring situations. *Peer tutoring* describes a form of peer-assisted learning in which learners of the same social standing help each other learn academic content or skills in paired or small group contexts. Librarians can train peer research consultants to use a variety of scaffolding techniques when helping other learners to improve their research skills. Peer research consultants can learn to assess learners' current research skills and use techniques such as modeling and joint note-taking to scaffold research assistance. Another good strategy is to ask questions that prompt their fellow learners to think critically about issues related to evidence, bias, and authority of sources. They can also draw upon their own research experiences, explain information literacy concepts in language that is familiar to other learners, and model the affective components of learning, such as speaking positively about their own past research projects.

....

IMPLICATIONS FOR LIBRARIES

When assisting learners in a variety of situations, librarians can provide guidance themselves, train others to provide learners with guidance, or provide resources that support different types of guidance.

Librarians can use some of the following strategies to integrate theory relating to instructional guidance into library services:

- Adjust the amount and type of assistance given during research and technology consultations based on a learner's responses, moving toward the end goal of having the learner complete the task on their own.
- Schedule drop-in clinics, in both in-person and online formats, that allow learners to get individual help with research and technology skills. Create handouts, web materials, and videos that provide support that learners can return to later to review the skills learned.
- Host events featuring representatives from various school or campus support services in which learners can meet and be paired with experts from a variety of areas (e.g., academic libraries can host research fairs in which graduate students can receive individual assistance from experts in writing, statistics, grants, etc.).
- Collaborate with other school or campus entities (e.g., writing centers, math centers) to hold tutoring sessions in the library.
- Hire students to provide peer assistance regarding research, technology, media, and makerspace skills.
- Provide instruction to tutors (e.g., how to begin and end a consultation, how to become familiar with the needs of the tutee, how to give feedback regarding correct and incorrect answers, and how to rescue a poor session). Continually monitor the work of tutors and provide feedback.
- Carefully prepare supporting materials for tutors and give them choices about how to integrate these materials into sessions. Ask tutors to create print or digital materials to support the work of other learners.
- Provide opportunities for interns and mentees to work with librarians and other staff members. Thoughtfully pair interns and mentees with staff members and implement some structure to guide their interactions. Have thoughtful conversations with interns and mentees to ensure that their learning and career goals are being addressed as much as possible.

TEACHING LIBRARIAN'S CORNER

Scaffolding is commonly used in library instruction in both individual and whole class contexts, although the term is sometimes used with different meanings. Because of the building metaphor that it employs, scaffolding has often been used to describe the sequencing of tasks so that they build upon each other, becoming progressively more difficult.

Librarians can use several strategies to provide scaffolding during individual and class instructional situations:

- Use initial assessments to gauge learners' knowledge and skill levels, and adjust instruction accordingly. The assessments can be formal or informal, written or verbal. Discuss and solicit learners' input about the content to be learned.
- Relate content to learners' interests or to familiar contexts. Ask questions that encourage learners to make connections to their own experiences. Reframe content or use simpler vocabulary to help learners understand.
- Highlight information or ask questions that focus on certain elements of a task. Break down more complex tasks into manageable components, and have learners complete the easier components first.
- Engage in mutual note-taking (e.g., write notes about resources and keywords on a handout and then encourage learners to add to it).
- Model how to approach a task and then ask learners to repeat it. Have learners complete certain tasks themselves with guidance (e.g., searching a database, editing an image).
- Use collaborative learning situations to enable learners to provide scaffolding or tutoring for each other.
- Provide constructive feedback that helps learners understand what they are doing well. Offer encouragement.
- Model or ask questions that encourage learners to summarize and reflect upon what they have learned.

Scaffolding and the Jigsaw Method

One pedagogical technique that enables learners to provide mutual scaffolding support in classroom contexts is the *jigsaw method*, a teaching strategy developed by Elliot Aronson that combines collaborative learning with peer instruction.[11] With the jigsaw method, ownership of certain tasks or topics is assigned to different group members, who learn and become proficient in their particular area. For example, learners can be responsible for learning to use different databases or tools, or for understanding different sources. Each learner then provides support for other group members as they learn that content. This method can also be modified based on the instructional need.

FURTHER READING

Falchikov, Nancy. *Learning Together: Peer Tutoring in Higher Education*. London: Routledge, 2001.

Rogoff, Barbara. *Apprenticeship in Thinking: Cognitive Development in Social Context*. New York: Oxford University Press, 1990.

Vygotsky, L. S. *Mind in Society: The Development of Higher Psychological Processes*. Edited by Michael Cole. Cambridge, MA: Harvard University Press, 1978.

QUESTIONS TO CONSIDER

1. How do the techniques of scaffolding and guided participation relate to the concept of the zone of proximal development? Provide an example of each in a library context.

2. How might scaffolding in a classroom situation differ from that in an individual consultation? Give some examples.

3. Imagine that you must make an argument to your library administration to implement a peer tutoring, teaching, or outreach program. What would the program look like? How would you make the argument?

NOTES

1. L. S. Vygotsky, *Mind in Society: The Development of Higher Psychological Processes*, ed. Michael Cole (Cambridge, MA: Harvard University Press, 1978), 86.

2. Vygotsky, *Mind in Society*, 84–91.

3. Vygotsky, *Mind in Society*, 86.

4. James V. Wertsch, *Vygotsky and the Social Formation of Mind* (Cambridge, MA: Harvard University Press, 1985).

5. L. S. Vygotsky, "The Development of Scientific Concepts in Childhood," in *The Collected Works of L. S. Vygotsky*, ed. Robert W. Rieber, trans. Marie J. Hall, vol. 1 (Springer, 1987), 209.

6. David Wood, Jerome S. Bruner, and Gail Ross, "The Role of Tutoring in Problem Solving," *Journal of Child Psychology and Psychiatry* 17, no. 2 (1976): 90, https://doi.org/10.1111/j.1469-7610.1976.tb00381.x.

7. Judith A. Langer and Arthur N. Applebee, "Reading and Writing Instruction: Toward a Theory of Teaching and Learning," *Review of Research in Education* 13 (1986): 171–94, https://doi.org/10.2307/1167222; Sadhana Puntambekar, "Scaffolding," in *Psychology of Classroom Learning: An Encyclopedia*, ed. Eric M. Anderman and Lynley H. Anderman, vol. 2, 2 vols. (Detroit: Gale Cengage Learning, 2009), 759–63; C. Addison Stone, "The Metaphor of Scaffolding: Its Utility for the Field of Learning Disabilities," *Journal of Learning Disabilities* 31, no. 4 (July 1, 1998): 344–64, https://doi.org/10.1177/002221949803100404.

8. Barbara Rogoff, *Apprenticeship in Thinking: Cognitive Development in Social Context* (New York: Oxford University Press, 1990), 18.

9. Rogoff, *Apprenticeship in Thinking*.

10. Barbara Rogoff, *The Cultural Nature of Human Development* (New York: Oxford University Press, 2003), 283–88; Rogoff, *Apprenticeship in Thinking*, 8–19.

11. Elliot Aronson, *The Jigsaw Classroom* (Beverly Hills, CA: Sage, 1978).

INDIVIDUAL DIFFERENCES

THEORETICAL OVERVIEW

Libraries are filled with people who learn in different ways. Some differences are related to fixed personality traits; others are a result of behaviors learned through cultural experiences. Some learner characteristics change with a person's age, ability, and level of development. Regardless, learners' individual differences will have an impact on their preferences for learning, their motivations to learn, and the strategies they use to tackle certain tasks. Librarians should consider individual differences when designing physical and digital spaces, choosing collections, or providing services.

Although there are numerous ways that people differ in learning and thinking, a few differences that are most influential or are best supported by evidence are described below. In addition, the theory of multiple types of intelligence, which reconsiders and challenges traditional views of intelligence, is also presented.

Learning Differences

Learners may differ in any number of ways, such as their personality traits or their *cognitive styles*, which describe different patterns of perceiving, processing information, and problem-solving.[1] However, the four learning differences described below should not be confused with learning styles theory, which not only explains distinctions in how people acquire knowledge and skills, but also suggests that learners will perform better if instruction is tailored to the ways they learn best.

For example, the popular "VAK" learning styles model classifies learners as either visual, auditory, or kinesthetic. This model indicates that people learn best when the content to be learned is presented in their preferred mode (e.g., visual learners are presented content through images, auditory learners are presented content through spoken text, etc.). However, a persistent lack of evidence supports this notion.[2]

Introverted and Extroverted Learners

One way to understand individual differences in learning revolves around the distinction between introverts and extroverts. Introversion describes a personality trait in which a person's energy is directed toward their inner world of thoughts, ideas, and reflections, while extroversion describes a trait in which energy is directed toward the outer world of people and activity.[3] Swiss psychoanalyst Carl Jung (1875–1961) was one of the first people to characterize these traits. While people can be classified as either extroverts or introverts, their traits can also be understood on a continuum, with some people having higher or lower degrees of the trait and others located somewhere in the middle.

Extroverts tend to be social, talkative, assertive, outgoing, energetic, and friendly. They are more task-oriented, more susceptible to social influences, and more easily distracted. In learning situations, extroverts tend to excel at learning tasks that involve activity, frequent feedback, and multimodal forms of communication. Introverts are often quiet, shy, reflective, reserved, and focused. They are motivated by personal values, often like to plan ahead, and enjoy focusing on concepts and ideas. Introverts tend to excel at learning tasks that involve organization and analysis, structured material, and time for reflection.[4]

Degrees of extroversion and introversion are thought to be affected by different arousal levels in specific neocortical areas of the brain. Extroverts have low levels of arousal and perform best in situations with more stimuli that generate their interest, while introverts have high levels of arousal and perform best in situations with less stimuli that allow them to focus. This difference often translates to a need for physical and social learning environments that allow for either greater or lesser amounts of stimulation and social interaction. Thus, extroverts enjoy open, noisier learning environments while introverts enjoy quieter, structured learning environments. Extroverts express a greater enjoyment of collaborative learning while introverts less so, although extroverts may also become more easily distracted by the social interaction that comes with group learning. In contrast, introverts are more likely to prefer to learn and study independently.[5]

Strategies for Teaching Quiet Learners

Teaching learners who appear to be quiet or introverted can sometimes be disconcerting, especially when a librarian asks a question of the class and no one responds. Are quiet learners unengaged? Are they confused? Or perhaps they are reflecting upon a potential response? Some learners are quiet because they are introverted, while others may be confused by the material, and still others might be embarrassed about speaking up and possibly being wrong in front of the class. Learners may be quiet for different reasons, but the following strategies can be helpful when teaching them:

- Wait for a bit after asking questions to give quiet learners time to think. Quiet learners often need time to formulate answers to questions.
- Incorporate different ways of participating (e.g., writing, taking notes, in-class activities), as quiet learners are sometimes reluctant to speak aloud in front of the whole class.
- Use technologies that help quiet learners to participate in class in an unintimidating manner (e.g., anonymous polling software, discussion boards in online classes).
- Encourage learners to speak with you outside of class in case they are uncomfortable asking questions in a whole class setting.
- Keep group sizes small during collaborative learning situations, as quiet learners may be reluctant to speak up in larger groups.
- Share strategies with learners for productive communication in small groups, so that quiet learners are not overrun by those who are more talkative.[6]

Reflective and Active Learners

Another way that learners differ is through a type of cognitive style, or pattern of thinking, known as *cognitive tempo*, which refers to an individual's tendency to respond to an information-processing situation with a more reflective or impulsive approach.[7] Reflection refers to the state of being thoughtful about one's actions and of considering alternatives before acting. Active or impulsive learners respond faster, evaluate their responses less carefully, and make more errors, while reflective learners respond more slowly, evaluate their responses more carefully, and make fewer errors.[8]

Active learners enjoy new situations and taking action, although they may act without sufficient preparation, get bored when following through on tasks, or take risks. They may enjoy practical applications, interacting with their environment, and influencing others. In learning situations, active learners may enjoy doing activities and learning collaboratively. Reflective learners may be better listeners and more methodical, but they may also lack assertiveness or be slower to make decisions. They may be interested in meaning, values, and understanding issues from different points of view. In learning situations, reflective learners may like reading, self-directed tasks, listening to lectures, or online learning.[9] Reflective learners may be more adept at metacognitive strategies that require them to be aware of their moods and strengths during learning. At the same time, active learners can become more reflective when time is set aside for processing, when they learn metacognitive skills, or when educators model reflective behaviors.[10]

The qualities of reflection and action are also related to introversion and extroversion, with introverts tending to be more reflective and extroverts tending to be more impulsive or action-oriented. In addition, children tend to be more impulsive when they are younger but become more reflective as they age.[11]

Abstract and Concrete Learners

Learners may also differ as to whether they employ a more abstract or concrete approach to perceiving, processing, and understanding information. Abstract learners approach information from a conceptual or theoretical perspective that is divorced from particular instances. Concrete learners approach information with reference to specific details and examples from the environment.[12]

Abstract learners are better at seeing the "big picture" and taking an objective approach to problem-solving. They use reason and intuition when approaching information, seek larger patterns among ideas, and are less dependent on environmental cues. They may be interested in ideas, theory, mathematics, and analysis. In learning situations, abstract thinkers may enjoy listening to lectures or engaging in independent, self-directed learning. Concrete learners are more practical, realistic, and focused on specific tasks. They may use tangible experiences to help them understand concepts, enjoy dealing with real-life situations, and enjoy relating to others. In learning situations, concrete thinkers may enjoy group work, projects, and discussion of real-world problems.[13]

The distinction between abstract and concrete learning shares some similarities with the types of cognitive styles called field dependence and field independence, which describe the importance of the setting or field in which stimuli occur for perceiving and understanding information.[14] Field independent learners are more conceptual and analytical, are less reliant on contextual clues to generate understanding, and are able to process information using their own organizational and structural patterns. In learning situations, field independent learners are more likely to enjoy independent learning and to excel at problem-solving and theoretical learning. In contrast, field dependent learners are more sensitive to the context of events for processing and understanding information. They are more oriented toward facts and specific circumstances, and they use external cues to help them structure and understand information. In learning situations, field dependent learners are more likely to enjoy collaborative and social learning environments in which the learning context is important. They also tend to do well with highly structured learning situations that involve the use of clear goals, directions, and feedback.[15] Field dependence/independence can be understood as a continuum, with most people falling somewhere between the two extremes. Young children are highly field dependent but become less so as they age.[16]

Visualizers and Verbalizers

Verbalizer/visualizer is a cognitive style that describes an individual's preference for receiving and processing information through either words or images. This characteristic of learners is based on Allan Paivio's theory of dual coding, which characterizes two different mental systems for processing verbal and pictorial information[17] (see chapter 4, "Multimedia").

Verbalizers prefer to learn through the printed or spoken word. In instructional situations, they may prefer reading and outlining information and may enjoy listening to lectures. Visualizers prefer to learn through graphics, drawings, illustrations, and maps. They may prefer reading text that contains images and enjoy interpreting graphs and charts. In instructional situations, they may enjoy using images or graphic organizers and learning through video games.[18]

While some learners demonstrate a preference for visual or verbal information, many show no preference and are comfortable learning through either type.[19] In addition, learners in either category may not always process information in one way or the other; instead, it is likely that learners adjust their information processing strategies depending on the type of task they are engaged in.[20] Finally, there may be variations within these categories as well. Among visualizers, for example, some—such as visual artists—enjoy using imagery to represent concrete representations of objects, while others—such as engineers—enjoy using imagery to represent and transform spatial relationships.[21]

Multiple Intelligences

In addition to the differences described above, the theory of multiple intelligences offers another way for librarians and other educators to understand how learners are unique. Howard Gardner, an educational psychologist, developed this theory in the 1980s in response to common, but limited, views of intelligence. Prior to the introduction of Gardner's theory, intelligence was largely believed to be related to the logical, mathematical, and linguistic skills associated with typical academic performance. Intelligence was also thought to be easily and concisely measured by the standard IQ test, which was developed in the early twentieth century.

Gardner defined intelligence as "an information-processing potential to solve problems or create products that are valued in at least one culture."[22] He identified eight different intelligences, each comprised of many different skills and each having a core set of operations (e.g., a core operation of people with high spatial intelligence is being good at navigation). Each intelligence is also encoded in symbol systems that are culturally derived methods of creating and sharing meaning (e.g., music is shared through systems of musical notation).[23]

Gardner identified eight different intelligences that are expressed in different ways and are associated with different neural patterns:

- *Linguistic intelligence:* the ability to understand and create products involving language, such as speech, reading, writing, and multimodal forms of communication
- *Logical mathematical intelligence:* the ability to make calculations, solve abstract problems, enact science, and strategize
- *Spatial intelligence:* the ability to use maps, work with objects, and create and work with visual products
- *Musical intelligence:* the ability to create and interpret different types of sound and musical patterns and combinations
- *Bodily-kinesthetic intelligence:* the ability to use one's body with awareness and control in activities such as sports, dance, or other physical endeavors
- *Interpersonal intelligence:* the ability to observe and understand other people's emotions and motivations, and to communicate with and lead others
- *Intrapersonal intelligence:* the ability and awareness to recognize and assess one's own feelings, skills, motivations, and intentions
- *Naturalistic intelligence:* the ability to recognize patterns and distinguish among products of the natural world such as animals, plants, and weather formations[24]

People possess a combination of intelligences in these eight different domains, and as a result, they may be more or less adept in each of the areas. While people have an innate aptitude for intelligence in particular areas, intelligences can also be developed through learning and practice.

Gardner's theory of multiple intelligences suggests that learners who may struggle in the traditional academic areas of reading, writing, and math that are commonly assessed through standardized tests may, in fact, be talented in other significant ways. Given this, librarians and other educators should use instructional strategies and activities that appeal to learners' different intelligences and give them choices about how they learn. These can provide different paths for learners to remember, understand, and apply what they learn, and can promote increased engagement in the learning process.

Finally, it is worth noting that Gardner derived his theory from a diverse set of research, theory, and narrative sources across a range of disciplines. This method of developing the theory has opened it up to critics who assert that it lacks a sufficient base of empirical support.[25] Nonetheless, Gardner's theory has had broad appeal in its critique of more constricted definitions of intelligence and has suggested a way of approaching instruction that librarians and other educators can use to develop lessons that engage and motivate different types of learners.

IMPLICATIONS FOR LIBRARIES

The ways that individuals differ in how they learn may factor into choices affecting a range of library activities, from space design to event planning to the provision of technologies. Specifically, introverts and extroverts may differ in their preferences for using library spaces, reflective and active learners may differ in their preferences for events, and verbalizers and visualizers may differ in their preferences for using certain media and technologies. Because learners possess different intelligences, they will also enjoy engaging in different kinds of activities.

Librarians can use some of the following strategies to provide support for different types of learners:

- Provide a variety of spaces for study and meeting, including spaces that allow for more stimulation and socialization and spaces that allow for quiet reflection.
- Make collections available that appeal to learners of multiple intelligences (e.g., maps, musical scores, books about the environment).
- Provide tools and technologies that allow learners to create content in a variety of ways, such as creating audio and video, building digital models and maps, and constructing mathematical calculations and simulations.
- Provide technologies that allow for different ways of interacting with, listening to, and viewing various media, including headphones and

assistive technologies. Ensure that technologies allow learners to listen to and view digital materials according to their needs (e.g., alter the size of text, turn sound off or on, etc.).

- Offer technology training that fosters learners' different strengths and intelligences (e.g., training in software for media creation, graphic design, or statistical analysis).
- Provide support in the library for completing projects or assignments that differ from traditional reading, writing, and math assignments (e.g., story maps, digital stories, posters, models).
- Ensure that library web content adheres to accessibility standards (e.g., can be interpreted by screen readers).
- Partner with school and community groups to bring programming into the library that supports multiple intelligences (e.g., nature programs, art projects, performances, science talks).
- Make items available for checkout that support creativity and exploration in different subject areas (e.g., items for making, science kits, art kits, anatomy models).
- Host events and put on exhibits that appeal to those with different intelligences (e.g., dance and musical performances, art exhibits, science exhibits).
- Provide physical and digital forums for presenting the projects of different types of learners (e.g., design projects, performances, story maps, videos, literary readings).

TEACHING LIBRARIAN'S CORNER

Librarians do not need to give each learner a personality test to understand how they might be unique; instead, librarians may simply find it helpful to become aware of the range of potential differences that might exist in any instructional situation. While it is impossible for librarians to simultaneously teach to every learner's unique characteristics, they can reach different types of learners by using a variety of pedagogical techniques and presenting information in diverse ways.

Librarians can use several strategies to teach with learning differences in mind:

- Share options with educators about alternatives to traditional research paper assignments (e.g., working in groups to create an online research guide that integrates text and images; taking an existing article and converting it to an image; creating a comparison chart showing key points from different sources).

- When working with educators, encourage them to give learners choices about different communication modes (e.g., creating audio or video, designing an infographic, writing a story or script) that they can use to complete a task or assignment to appeal to their different strengths and preferences.

- Design lessons that consist of different components to appeal to different learners (e.g., small group discussion, reflective writing, and hands-on learning activities in different areas of the library, such as book stacks, special collections, and makerspaces).

- When giving lectures (which appeal to some learners but not others), integrate them with thought-provoking questions, examples, activities, images, and videos.

- When activities or tasks can be done equally well by individuals or groups, give learners an option for how they want to complete them.

- When assigning large group projects, allow learners to assume different roles within the project (e.g., writer, illustrator, etc.) and share examples of how to do that. Share these techniques with educators.

- Ask learners to create visual representations of a research topic or their research process.

- Have learners take a primary source document such as a newspaper article, oral interview script, or scientific study and transform it into another format of their choice, such as a letter, script, poem, song, poster, or brochure.

- Integrate opportunities for learners to reflect upon their own learning strengths, preferences, and intelligences.

Universal Design for Learning

Universal design for learning (UDL) is a framework that attempts to make learning as accessible and inclusive as possible to as many different learners as possible. UDL is based upon the concept of universal design, an approach to architecture, communication, and product design that emphasizes the importance of usability and accessibility to the fullest extent possible. UDL advocates using several strategies to both support and challenge learners of various abilities, preferences, and cultural and linguistic backgrounds, and it often includes attention to the use of technologies to meet different

(continued)

learning needs. UDL is based on three major principles described by the nonprofit educational organization called CAST (formerly the Center for Applied Special Technology):

1. Provide multiple means of engagement to address the "why" of learning. This includes giving learners autonomy, using authentic learning tasks, and fostering motivation and reflection.
2. Provide multiple means of representation to address the "what" of learning. This includes using different media to represent content and using strategies to help learners understand and process information.
3. Provide multiple means of expression to address the "how" of learning. This includes allowing learners to use various media and tools to complete tasks and teaching strategies for goal-setting, planning, and monitoring.[26]

Librarians can use these principles to aid in their design of lessons and assignments and in their creation of learning materials in both in-person and online instructional situations.

FURTHER READING

Gardner, Howard. *Frames of Mind: The Theory of Multiple Intelligences*. 3rd ed. New York: Basic Books, 2011.

Hall, Tracey E., Anne Meyer, and David H. Rose. *Universal Design for Learning in the Classroom: Practical Applications*. New York: Guilford, 2012.

Jonassen, David H., and Barbara L. Grabowski, eds. *Handbook of Individual Differences, Learning, and Instruction*. Hillsdale, NJ: Routledge, 1993.

QUESTIONS TO CONSIDER

1. Reflect upon your own learning characteristics. How do you like to learn? How does this affect your use of spaces and technologies, as well as your own learning strategies?

2. Pick a library of your choosing and visit it in person or online. How might the objects, collections, events, and spaces in that library appeal to learners of different intelligences?

3. Take a lesson about an information literacy or other topic and identify aspects of the lesson that address the why, what, and how of learning. What strategies can you incorporate from the universal design for learning framework to appeal to different learners?

NOTES

1. Simon Cassidy, "Learning Styles: An Overview of Theories, Models, and Measures," *Educational Psychology* 24, no. 4 (2004): 419–44; David H. Jonassen and Barbara L. Grabowski, *Handbook of Individual Differences, Learning, and Instruction* (Hillsdale, NJ: Routledge, 1993), 173–75.

2. Vicki Snider, *Myths and Misconceptions about Teaching: What Really Happens in the Classroom* (Lanham, MD: Rowman & Littlefield Education, 2006), 106–24; John G. Sharp, Rob Bowker, and Jenny Byrne, "VAK or VAK-uous? Towards the Trivialisation of Learning and the Death of Scholarship," *Research Papers in Education* 23, no. 3 (September 1, 2008): 293–314, https://doi.org/10.1080/02671520701755416; Philip M. Newton, "The Learning Styles Myth Is Thriving in Higher Education," *Frontiers in Psychology* 6 (December 15, 2015): 1–5, https://doi.org/10.3389/fpsyg.2015.01908.

3. "Introversion," in *APA Dictionary of Psychology,* ed. Gary R. VandenBos, 2nd ed. (Washington, DC: American Psychological Association, 2015), 561.

4. Jonassen and Grabowski, *Handbook of Individual Differences,* 367–79.

5. Ann Medaille and Janet Usinger, "'That's Going to Be the Hardest Thing for Me': Tensions Experienced by Quiet Students during Collaborative Learning Situations," *Educational Studies* 46, no. 2 (March 3, 2020): 240–57, https://doi.org/10.1080/030 55698.2018.1555456.

6. Ann Medaille and Janet Usinger, "Engaging Quiet Students in the College Classroom," *College Teaching* 67, no. 2 (April 3, 2019): 130–37, https://doi.org/10.1080/8 7567555.2019.1579701.

7. Jonassen and Grabowski, *Handbook of Individual Differences,* 113.

8. Jonassen and Grabowski, *Handbook of Individual Differences,* 113–25; Robert J. Sternberg and Elena L. Grigorenko, "Are Cognitive Styles Still in Style?" *The American Psychologist* 52, no. 7 (1997): 700–12, https://doi.org/10.1037/0003-066X.52.7.700.

9. Jonassen and Grabowski, *Handbook of Individual Differences,* 113–25; Frank Coffield et al., "Learning Styles and Pedagogy in Post-16 Learning: A Systematic and Critical Review," Learning & Skills Research Centre, 2004, 72; David A. Kolb, *Experiential Learning: Experience as the Source of Learning and Development,* 2nd ed. (Pearson, 2014), 104–10.

10. Jonassen and Grabowski, *Handbook of Individual Differences,* 113–25.

11. Jonassen and Grabowski, *Handbook of Individual Differences,* 113–25.

12. Jonassen and Grabowski, *Handbook of Individual Differences,* 249.

13. Kolb, *Experiential Learning,* 104–10; Coffield et al., "Learning Styles and Pedagogy in Post-16 Learning," 72; Jonassen and Grabowski, *Handbook of Individual Differences,* 249, 289.

14. Jonassen and Grabowski, *Handbook of Individual Differences,* 87.

15. Jonassen and Grabowski, *Handbook of Individual Differences*, 87–103; Herman A. Witkin, *Cognitive Styles, Essence and Origins: Field Dependence and Field Independence* (New York: International Universities Press, 1981).

16. Jonassen and Grabowski, *Handbook of Individual Differences*, 88.

17. Jonassen and Grabowski, *Handbook of Individual Differences*, 191.

18. Jonassen and Grabowski, *Handbook of Individual Differences*, 191–98.

19. Jonassen and Grabowski, *Handbook of Individual Differences*, 191.

20. Alan Richardson, "Verbalizer-Visualizer: A Cognitive Style Dimension," *Journal of Mental Imagery* 1, no. 1 (1977): 109–25.

21. Maria Kozhevnikov, "Cognitive Styles in the Context of Modern Psychology: Toward an Integrated Framework of Cognitive Style," *Psychological Bulletin* 133, no. 3 (2007): 464–81, https://doi.org/10.1037/0033-2909.133.3.464.

22. Howard E. Gardner, *Multiple Intelligences: New Horizons in Theory and Practice* (New York: Basic Books, 2008), 235.

23. Gardner, *Multiple Intelligences*, 6–8.

24. Howard Gardner, *Frames of Mind: The Theory of Multiple Intelligences*, 3rd ed. (New York: Basic Books, 2011); Scott Seider and Howard Gardner, "Multiple Intelligences," in *Psychology of Classroom Learning: An Encyclopedia*, ed. Eric M. Anderman and Lynley H. Anderman, vol. 2, 2 vols. (Detroit: Gale Cengage Learning, 2009), 635–38; Branton Shearer, "Multiple Intelligences in Teaching and Education: Lessons Learned from Neuroscience," *Journal of Intelligence* 6, no. 3 (2018): 38–45, https://doi.org/10.3390/jintelligence6030038.

25. Lynn Waterhouse, "Inadequate Evidence for Multiple Intelligences, Mozart Effect, and Emotional Intelligence Theories," *Educational Psychologist* 41, no. 4 (2006): 247–55, https://doi.org/10.1207/s15326985ep4104_5.

26. Tracey E. Hall, Anne Meyer, and David H. Rose, *Universal Design for Learning in the Classroom: Practical Applications* (New York: Guilford, 2012); CAST, "Universal Design for Learning Guidelines, Version 2.2," 2018, https://udlguidelines.cast.org/?utm_source=castsite&lutm_medium=web&utm_campaign=none&utm_content=aboutudl.

CONCLUSION

THE THEORIES PRESENTED IN THIS BOOK FIT TOGETHER LIKE PIECES IN A PUZ-
zle to create a larger picture of the phenomenon of learning. While the theories were described in relation to certain topics, most of them apply to many different aspects of the learning process. To illustrate, the theory of self-efficacy was addressed in the chapter on observation, but it has important implications for motivation, self-regulation, affect, and other topics as well. Information processing theory and Gagné's nine phases of learning were described in the chapter on attention, but they apply to many areas of teaching and learning, including the ways that materials are presented, and lessons are designed to help learners best understand, remember, and transfer what they learn to other situations.

Taken together, these theories suggest several overarching considerations for librarians as they think about ways to support learning. First, learning involves *engagement* on the part of the learner. Learners must be motivated in order to experience deep learning, and learning is strongly affected by emotional states. Learners are often interested in learning about topics that are relevant to their lives and that excite their imaginations. They must also have some awareness of their own thinking and learning processes and be partially able to direct their own learning so that they can capitalize on their individual preferences and passions. However, even though learning requires personal commitment and self-regulation, most learners need assistance to tap into their own motivations and to master self-regulatory strategies that can help them to become better learners. *Librarians can promote engagement in learning and help learners to direct and regulate their own learning processes.*

Second, these theories suggest that learning is an *active process* on the part of the learner. In order for learning to occur, learners must actively construct their own understandings; passively receiving information does not result in meaningful and lasting learning. Learners must participate in mental activities that allow them to explain, connect, analyze, compare, question, challenge, organize, evaluate, and so on. Learners can do this by discussing, collaborating, exploring, planning, conducting inquiries, making objects, or doing numerous other activities that allow for substantial mental processing. *Librarians can create learning situations that allow for active and deep mental involvement.*

Third, the *social, cultural, and physical environment* plays a significant role in learning. People often learn by observing the behaviors of those around them, by absorbing implicit cultural messages from their environment, by interacting with the materials and resources available to them, and by participating in activities within specific social contexts. Collaborating with peers, experts, and educators can often enhance learning by providing opportunities for joint problem-solving and dialogue, which enables learners to absorb different points of view and generate shared understandings. However, the environment can also serve as a source of distraction for learners or pose challenges that make learning difficult, so environmental factors have to be managed with care. *Librarians can arrange environments that contain resources and situations that enhance learning.*

Fourth, most learners benefit from having *guidance from an educator* to help them develop their thinking processes and learn knowledge and skills. While learners can achieve a certain amount on their own, educators are required to assess learners' needs, develop appropriate learning goals, design instructional sequences, and provide proper scaffolding. Because learning occurs differently in the mind of each individual, educators should adjust their assistance on the basis of learners' distinct needs, as determined by their ages, abilities, intelligences, interests, levels of motivation, and personalities. *Librarians can provide instructional guidance that recognizes the needs of different learners.*

Finally, learning can be enhanced when *instruction is designed and directed.* Thoughtful instructional design that is based in established theories can improve learning. Instruction can include a variety of tasks to maintain learners' attention, increase their motivation and curiosity, and ensure that different types of learners are engaged. Instructional situations can be designed to ensure that learners experience opportunities to develop higher-level and critical thinking skills through analysis, evaluation, inquiry, and creativity. While some learning situations may call for open-ended exploration, others require explicit direction. In addition, learners need considerable assistance in knowing what kinds of messages to attend to, so instructional resources, materials, and technologies should be used deliberately to ensure that a focus is maintained on learning goals. *Librarians can design instructional situations to provide varied and directed learning experiences, make the best use of instructional tools and resources, and maintain a focus on learning outcomes.*

These five considerations demonstrate some of the ways that the learning theories described in this book can be understood collectively. These considerations may also provide some guidance for librarians as they reflect upon their own approaches to supporting learning. If librarians understand theories like the ones described in this book, they do not have to rely on their best guesses when designing situations and environments that enhance learning. Learning theories can help librarians to engage in more meaningful and rewarding work, as helping others learn is at the core of what librarians do.

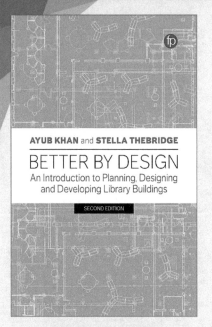
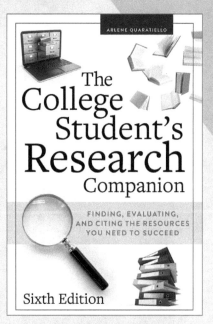

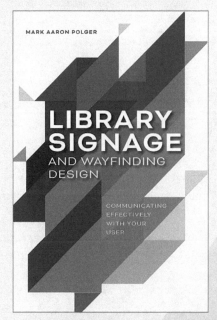